APPETIZERS
ON THE GRILL

*Innovative Hors d'Oeuvres,
Pizzas, Gourmet Sandwiches,
and Light Entrees*

BARBARA GRUNES

CHICAGO
REVIEW
PRESS

Library of Congress Cataloging-in-Publication Data

Grunes, Barbara
    Appetizers on the grill : innovative hors d'oeuvres, pizzas, gourmet sandwiches, and light entrees / Barbara Grunes. —1st ed.
        p.   cm.
        Includes index.
        ISBN 1-55652-145-6 : $9.95
        1. Appetizers.   2. Grilling.   I. Title.
TX740.G78   1992
641.8'12—dc20   92-2689
                                                                                      CIP

For my special friend Eunice Tobin, who first encouraged me in my first professional cooking effort: "You get ready and I'll get the students," she said.

Cover Photographer: Tim Turner

        1   2   3   4   5   6   7   8   9   10

Published in 1992 by Chicago Review Press, Incorporated
814 North Franklin Street, Chicago, Illinois 60610

ISBN 1-55652-145-6

CONTENTS

INTRODUCTION

As a cookbook author who is also a wife and mother, I am aware of the need for more light and easy menu options. Like many of you, I have found it necessary to balance my desire for fun and flavorful foods with an increased concern for eating more healthful foods. The solution for me has been the use of appetizers in my meal planning, not only as hors d'oeuvres but also as light entrees.

When grilling, many people do not even consider preparing appetizers. But the truth is that they are easy and quick, and once you have your grill started—why not? They are a delightful addition to a meal when you're entertaining family or friends, and they make a nice diversion while guests are waiting for the main meal to be prepared.

As a meal in themselves, appetizers are perfect for a backyard party or an informal get-together, yet they are elegant and fashionable enough for formal entertaining. And as a light summer menu alternative, there's nothing better.

Because of the mechanics of grilling, foods prepared in this way tend to be lighter and contain less fat. In these recipes I call for margarine or butter and give as an alternative to canola oil other oils. I have tried whenever possible to use more herbs for seasoning instead of salt and to suggest leaner cuts of meat eaten in smaller portions. For the recipes that call for creamy ingredients such as mayonnaise, sour cream, or cream cheese, you can use the reduced-fat, lower-calorie versions of these. More of your guests will be able to enjoy your grilled appetizers if you opt for the healthy alternatives. Of course there are some cheese recipes and certain recipes for special occasions when a splurge is called for.

Part of the appeal of grilling food is that it combines the best of the old and the new. It's a time-honored, proven way to produce delicious cooked dishes, and recent innovations in equipment and techniques have given it modern-day panache. The grill rack, for example, which I have used in most of the recipes for this book, is a convenient tool that makes it easy to grill all kinds of food without having the food stick or fall through into the coals. Then there's the pizza stone, which I found to be such a wonderful invention that I decided to devote an entire chapter to pizza on the grill.

So as long as you're going to grill your entree, it makes sense to grill your appetizers, too. As always, I advise you to have fun when grilling and not to be afraid of experimenting. Be creative, give each of these recipes your own personal touch, and, above all, enjoy.

HINTS FOR BETTER GRILLING

For dramatic grilling and extra flavor, sprinkle about ½ cup soaked and drained herbs over the hot coals before you grill. Match the herbs to the food you are grilling—for example, oregano for grilling pizza.

To grill using the **direct method,** mound coals in the center of the grill. Light the coals. After they are an ashen color, spread them out. Don't be hasty; if coals are not heated completely, grilling time will be affected. The recipes in this book use the direct method unless otherwise specified.

The **indirect method** of grilling is used for large cuts of meat. To prepare the grill for the indirect method, arrange the coals around a flat pan in the grill. Light the coals. When they are hot, fill the pan with hot water. The water imparts moisture and mellow flavor to the food. Indirect grilling is used most commonly for fatty foods when frequent grease flare-ups are not desirable. It also works best used with a covered grill. Indirect grilling takes longer, however, and the food usually doesn't brown as well.

When using a **smoker,** prepare it according to the manufacturer's directions. Always use hardwood charcoal for best results. Check the smoker after 1 hour to see if more coals or water is needed.

Keep in mind that much of the preparation for recipes in this book can be done in advance. And most of the recipes can easily be doubled. Don't wait for the last minute to start working. Have fun with your guests!

Tools and Accessories

It almost goes without saying that long-handled utensils are a must when grilling. Tongs, forks, spatulas, and brushes are all important items to have nearby when cooking over a hot grill. Spare no expense when you buy grill implements; quality products will serve you better and last longer.

Heavy mitts are very helpful when working around a hot grill or handling hot food, so they are also well worth an investment.

A spray bottle filled with water should also be at hand. When flare-ups occur, just spray water at the base of the flame until the fire is controlled, being careful not to extinguish the coals.

A supply of good-quality heavy-duty aluminum foil is indispensable. You can cover the bottom of your grill with foil to facilitate cleanup. Or use it to line your grill when cooking soft foods that might tend to break or fall into the fire; just make sure you punch a few holes in the foil to allow any grease to drip through. Aluminum foil can also be used to make an improvised lid for an uncovered brazier.

Griffo-Grill

While developing and testing the recipes in this book, I experimented with a considerable number of outdoor grilling accessories and products. One company, Griffo-Grill of Quincy, Illinois, whose products I had used with great success previously, expanded its product line, and I was delighted to find that the versatile Griffo-Grill rack provided the perfect tool for many of the appetizer recipes I have presented in this book. The grill rack fits directly on the grill, preventing small and soft pieces of food from falling through the grill onto the hot coals. The grill rack enables you to barbecue delicate seafood, smaller cuts such as fish or meat strips, and small vegetables such as jalapeño peppers or mushrooms with perfect ease. It is perfect for grilling onions, fruit slices, kabobs, and myriad other foods that can be tricky without a rack.

Here are a few suggestions for making the most of a Griffo-Grill rack:

- Oil the grill rack with vegetable oil or vegetable oil spray before use.

- To get better grill marks, place the rack on your grill for 5 to 10 minutes before cooking to preheat the grill to searing level.

- Use a nonabrasive brush rather than a regular grill brush to clean your grill rack.

Pizza Stone and Paddle

Pizza stones (or tiles), available at cookware stores and many department stores, make it possible to bake pizzas directly on the grill. I've tried various brands and found them all good. A pizza paddle is helpful for sliding the pizzas onto the heated stones. I put the stones over direct heat and let them get hot before adding the pizzas.

Fuels

Hardwood

Always avoid soft, resinous woods such as pine, spruce, and cedar. The smoke from these woods may seem pleasant on a cold winter evening, but it tends to give food an unpleasant taste. Also, do not use lumber or plywood; often such wood is treated with chemicals that may be harmful and certainly will not enhance the grilling experience. You can pick wood twigs from your garden or refer to the shopping sources listed in this book.

Charcoal

Charcoal comes in two varieties: lump, or hardwood, charcoal and briquettes.

Lump charcoal is made from whole pieces of wood and contains no additives or fillers. It burns cleanly and adds a pleasant yet subtle flavor to foods. This flavor will tend to vary depending on the type of wood from which the charcoal was made. Lump charcoal burns slowly and efficiently. Because it is pure, it has a low ash content.

Briquettes are made from wood scraps and sawdust. Filler and binders are added, and the charcoal is then pressed into briquette shapes. Briquettes work fine for my recipes, but I prefer to use lump charcoal.

Starters

Kindling

A good supply of dry kindling or solid starting material can save you a lot of trouble when preparing a fire. Arrange dry twigs, newspapers, or other flammable materials loosely and then cover with the appropriate amount of charcoal. Make sure that there is plenty of room for air to flow through the kindling and charcoal and that all vents are open so that the fire will have enough oxygen and will start quickly.

Always use only materials that will burn off cleanly and not leave any residue that might produce an undesirable taste in the food. In other words, I don't recommend lighter fluid.

Electric

Electric starters are easy to obtain and not overly expensive. They usually consist of an oval or oblong heating element that is used to start the charcoal. Once the coals begin to glow hot (normally within the first 10 minutes), the electric starter should be removed to prevent damage to the heating element.

One drawback to this type of starter is that it requires a nearby electrical outlet. Also, it can start only those coals that are touching the heating element, so you'll have to allow some extra time for the fire to spread throughout the rest of the charcoal. Otherwise, electric starters are durable, efficient, economical, and safe—and highly recommended.

Flue/Chimney

A flue or chimney is a cylinder of sheet metal that can be used quickly and effectively to start a charcoal fire. Its bottom is made of metal grates with vents located at intervals around the base. Usually it has a handle covered in wood or some other material that will remain cool while the chimney is in use.

To start a fire with a chimney, spread a layer of newspaper over the bottom grate. Be sure that all the vents are open and unobstructed and then fill the chimney three-quarters full of charcoal. The draft created by the burning newspaper will draw the fire upward through the charcoal, igniting it completely and efficiently. When the coals are ready, carefully pour them into the bottom of your grill and arrange as desired.

One drawback to this type of starter is that the chimney may not hold enough coals for a large fire. This can be overcome quite easily by simply adding extra charcoal to the burning coals and allowing a little longer to prepare the fire.

SHOPPING/MAIL-ORDER SOURCES

Carolyn Collins Caviar
PO Box 662
Crystal Lake, IL 60014
815-459-6210

The Chef's Catalog
3215 Commercial Ave.
Northbrook, IL 60062
312-480-9400

Crate & Barrel
725 Landwehr Rd.
Northbrook, IL 60062
800-323-5461

Gamatech
PO Box 8069
San Jose, CA 05155
408-291-5220

Griffo-Grill
301 Oak St.
Quincy, IL 62301
217-222-0779

Jessica's Biscuits
PO Box 301
Newtonville, MA 02160
617-965-0530

Nature's Own
453 S. Main St.
Attleboro, MA
508-226-4710

The Oriental Food Market
2801 W. Howard St.
Chicago, IL 60645
312-274-2826

Wild Game Inc.
2315 W. Huron St.
Chicago, IL 60612
312-278-1661

Williams-Sonoma
100 North Point St.
San Francisco, CA 94133
800-541-2233

PIZZA

Grilling pizza is new to most of us, but it actually comes from an old technique. After all, the very best tasting pizza is prepared in a wood-burning oven, so the transition to the grill is both natural and easy. For best results, one should remember a few tips: the stones (or "tiles") should always be preheated, and use a pizza paddle sprinkled with cornmeal for easy handling. The coals should preheat for about 20 minutes, then place your tiles on their tray on the grill's grate. Preheat the tiles until they're hot, about 10 minutes. Then slide your pizzas onto the tiles.

You can prepare your crust ahead of time, early in the day, and leave it refrigerated (wrapped in aluminum foil) until grilling time. Or roll out your pizza dough and cover and freeze it. Defrost and "decorate" your pizza when you light the coals.

Individual Mushroom Pizzas

Frozen bread dough is available at supermarkets.

8 servings

2	loaves frozen bread dough, defrosted and divided into 8 equal pieces

Topping

	Olive oil for brushing pizza
¾	pound goat cheese, crumbled
2	tablespoons fennel seeds
1	cup pine nuts
3	cups sliced button mushrooms, brown mushrooms, or wild mushrooms
½	cup grated Asiago cheese

On a lightly floured board, pat each piece of dough into a 7- or 8-inch circle. Brush dough with oil. Sprinkle dough with goat cheese, fennel, pine nuts, mushrooms, and cheese.

When the coals are hot, place the barbecue pizza tray, set with tiles, on the grill. Make sure tiles are hot before adding pizza. Shift pizzas onto a paddle, two at a time, and slide them onto the heated tiles. You can cook four pizzas at a time. Or if your grill is too small, cook two pizzas and refrigerate the remaining two pizzas until the first two are done. Cover grill and cook for about 10 minutes. When pizza is cooked, crust will be firm and toppings hot.

Using a pizza paddle and a long-handled spatula, quickly push pizzas onto paddle and from there onto individual serving dishes at the table. Serve hot.

Pizza with Sausage
and Red Peppers

You can sprinkle your pizza paddle with cornmeal to help slide the pizza from the paddle to the hot stone or tiles. If you're in a hurry, use a prepared tomato puree—but nothing really compares with homemade sauce.

8 servings

Dough (2 12-inch crusts)

1	cup warm water
½	teaspoon honey
1	¼-ounce package active dry yeast
2¼ to 3	cups all-purpose flour
½	teaspoon salt
3	tablespoons olive oil

Rosemary/Basil Sauce (1 quart sauce)

1	6-ounce can tomato paste
1	28-ounce can tomatoes, including liquid, pureed
½	cup water
1	tablespoon dried oregano
1	teaspoon dried basil
½	teaspoon dried rosemary
½	teaspoon garlic powder
¼	teaspoon salt
¼	teaspoon freshly ground pepper
¼	cup minced fresh parsley

Topping

Olive oil for brushing pizza
¼   pound precooked sweet Italian sausage, casing removed, crumbled
1   large red bell pepper, seeded and sliced thin
1   cup grated mozzarella cheese

Mix honey into warm water in small bowl or measuring cup. Dissolve yeast. Let mixture stand for about 4 to 6 minutes or until yeast begins to bubble.

Using a mixer with a dough hook or a food processor fitted with the steel blade, combine 2 cups flour, salt, and oil. Add yeast mixture and enough flour to make a soft, almost sticky dough. Mix dough ingredients for a few seconds in a food processor or about 1 to 2 minutes in an electric mixer. Dough will be soft and sticky. Gather dough into a ball and knead three or four times on a floured board.

Gather dough into a ball and set in a bowl; cover lightly with a towel or aluminum foil. Place in a draft-free area for 1 hour or until dough doubles in size. Divide dough in half. Shape dough into a 12-inch circle by pressing it with the floured heel of your hand or by using a rolling pin. Place it on a pizza paddle and cover lightly again. The second rising time should be 15 minutes.

While the dough is rising a second time, prepare the sauce. Combine tomato paste, pureed tomatoes, and water in a medium saucepan. Stir remaining sauce ingredients and simmer for 10 minutes, stirring occasionally. Cool.

To assemble, brush pizza dough lightly with oil. Spoon sauce over crust. With the back of a spoon, spread to within ½ inch of edges. Sprinkle sausage, red pepper, and cheese over pizza.

When the coals are hot, place the pizza stone or tiles on the grill. Make sure tiles are hot before adding pizza. Shift pizza onto a paddle and slide it onto the heated tiles.

Cover grill and cook for 5 to 10 minutes or until done. When pizza is cooked, its crust will be firm and the cheese melted.

Using a pizza paddle and a long-handled spatula, quickly push pizza onto paddle and from there onto a serving dish. Cut into wedges or squares. Serve hot.

Individual Thin-Crust Vegetable Pizzas

8 servings

1	recipe pizza dough (see Index)
	Olive oil for brushing dough
1	cup chopped blanched broccoli
1	medium-sized onion, chopped
1	medium-sized green pepper, seeded and chopped
1	cup thinly sliced mushrooms
1½	cups grated mozzarella cheese
4	cloves garlic, minced
1	tablespoon dried basil

After dough has risen, shape it into four 8-inch circles as described in preceding recipe. Each crust will be about ¼ inch thick. Place crusts on a cookie sheet.

Brush dough lightly with oil. Sprinkle with broccoli, onion, bell pepper, and mushrooms. Sprinkle with mozzarella cheese, leaving a ½-inch border. Sprinkle pizza with garlic and basil. Use two spatulas to move each pizza from the cookie sheet to the pizza tiles. Refrigerate the pizzas that are not on the grill.

When the coals are hot, place the tiles on their tray on the grill. Make sure tiles are hot before adding pizza. Shift pizzas onto a paddle, two at a time, and slide them onto heated tiles. Cover grill and cook for about 10 minutes or until done. When pizza is cooked, crust will be firm and toppings hot.

Using a pizza paddle and a long-handled spatula, quickly push pizzas onto paddle and from there onto individual serving dishes at the table. Serve hot.

Whole-Wheat Pita Bread
Seafood Pizza

6 servings

3	whole-wheat pita breads, each split into 2 rounds
	Olive oil for brushing pita bread
2	cups Rosemary/Basil Sauce (see Index) or prepared tomato sauce
24	large shrimp, peeled, deveined, and cut in half lengthwise
2	cups bay scallops
3	scallions, chopped

Brush pita bread rounds lightly with oil. Brush sauce over bread. Sprinkle shrimp, scallops, and scallions over sauce.

When the coals are hot, place the barbecue pizza tray, set with tiles, on the grill. Make sure tiles are hot before adding pizza. Shift pizzas onto a paddle and slide them onto the heated tiles. You can cook three pizzas together. Cover grill and cook pizzas for 2 to 3 minutes or until done. Pizza is cooked when crust is toasted but not burned.

Using a pizza paddle and a long-handled spatula, quickly push pizzas onto paddle and from there onto individual dishes at the table. Serve hot.

Anchovy and Onion Pizza

8 servings

½ recipe pizza dough (see Index) or 1 10-inch prepared pizza crust
3 tablespoons olive oil
2 cloves garlic, minced
3 medium-sized onions, sliced
¼ teaspoon salt
¼ teaspoon freshly ground pepper
½ teaspoon fennel seeds
3 large tomatoes, sliced thin
1 2-ounce can flat anchovy fillets, drained
½ cup sliced pitted black olives
   Olive oil for brushing pizza edges

After dough has risen, shape it into a 10-inch circle on a pizza paddle by rolling it out or shaping it with the floured heels of your hands. Set aside.

Heat 3 tablespoons olive oil in a frying pan. Add garlic and onions and sauté over medium heat for 4 minutes, stirring occasionally. Season with salt, pepper, and fennel. Set aside to cool.

To assemble, arrange tomatoes, slightly overlapping, over the dough. Spread the onion mixture over the tomatoes. Add the anchovies in rows or in an X design. Sprinkle pizza with olives. Brush edges of pizza with oil.

When the coals are hot, place the barbecue pizza tray, set with tiles, on the grill. Make sure tiles are hot before adding pizza. Shift pizza onto a paddle and slide it onto the heated tiles.

Cover grill and cook for 5 to 10 minutes or until done. When pizza is cooked, crust will be firm and toppings hot.

Using a pizza paddle and a long-handled spatula, quickly push pizza onto paddle and from there onto a serving dish. Cut into wedges or squares. Serve hot.

Focaccia

Focaccia is a pizza-style bread cooked and served right from the skillet.

8 servings

>　　Olive oil for brushing pan and focaccia
> 1　recipe pizza dough (see Index)
> 8　rehydrated sun-dried tomatoes, chopped
> 2　scallions, chopped
> 1½　teaspoons dried basil

Brush a 9-inch cast-iron skillet with oil. With floured hands, push prepared dough evenly into the pan. With fingers, punch about 10 evenly spaced indentations in the dough. Brush dough lightly with oil. Sprinkle tomatoes, scallions, and basil over dough.

When the coals are hot, place the barbecue pizza tray, set with tiles, on the grill. Make sure tiles are hot before adding skillet. Place focaccia on heated tiles. Cover grill and cook for 10 to 15 minutes. Focaccia is done when dough is firm to the touch. A tester inserted in the dough will come out dry.

Set focaccia on buffet and cut into serving-sized pieces. Serve hot or warm.

English Muffin Pizza
with Two Toppings

I fondly remember my mother preparing this recipe for the family and guests. Making this pizza on the grill adds a crispness and a smoky flavor. Each topping recipe makes enough for four muffins.

4 servings

Topping I

1	cup Rosemary/Basil Sauce (see Index) or prepared tomato sauce
1	tomato, sliced
1	cup grated mozzarella cheese
1	teaspoon dried oregano

Topping II

1	cup chutney
½	cup cream cheese at room temperature
¼	teaspoon ground cumin
4	English muffins, split

For the first topping, spoon tomato sauce over cut side of muffins, spreading it with the back of a spoon. Set a slice of tomato on top and sprinkle with cheese and oregano.

For the second topping, combine chutney, cream cheese, and cumin. Spread mixture over cut side of the muffins.

When the coals are hot, place the barbecue pizza tray, set with tiles, on the grill. Make sure tiles are hot before adding muffins. Place the muffins on the heated tiles. Cover grill and cook for 2 minutes or until muffins are toasted and toppings hot.

Transfer muffins to serving dish. You may want to cut them into quarters and pass them on a tray. Serve hot.

Individual French Bread Chicago Pizzas

Chicagoans take their pizza seriously and feel strongly that their city should be called the "pizza capital of the world." This recipe is an adaptation of the Windy City's famous deep-dish pizza. Chicagoans serve three condiments to sprinkle on pizza: hot red pepper flakes, crumbled oregano, and freshly grated Parmesan cheese.

8 servings

3	tablespoons olive oil
2	medium-sized onions, chopped
3	cloves garlic, minced
1	28-ounce can tomatoes, including liquid, pureed
1	6-ounce can tomato paste
½	cup water
1	tablespoon dried oregano
1	teaspoon dried basil
1	teaspoon honey
¼	teaspoon fennel seeds
½	teaspoon salt
¼	teaspoon freshly ground pepper
4	individual French bread rolls, cut in half lengthwise
1½	cups grated mozzarella cheese
½	cup freshly grated Parmesan or Asiago cheese
½	cup hot red pepper flakes for garnish
½	cup dried oregano for garnish
	Freshly grated Parmesan cheese for garnish

For sauce, heat oil in a medium saucepan. Add onion and garlic and sauté for 4 minutes, stirring occasionally. Mix in tomato puree, tomato paste, water, oregano, basil, honey, fennel, salt, and pepper. Reduce heat to simmer and continue cooking for 10 minutes, stirring occasionally. Cool sauce.

To assemble pizzas, brush cut side of rolls generously with sauce. Sprinkle with cheeses.

When the coals are hot, place the barbecue pizza tray, set with tiles, on the grill. Place the pizzas on the heated tiles. Cover grill and cook for 2 to 3 minutes. When pizza is cooked, bread will be toasted and cheese melted.

Transfer pizzas to a serving platter. Serve with bowls of red pepper flakes, oregano, and Parmesan cheese.

VEGETABLES

Skewered Potatoes
with Freshwater Caviar

Feel free to use reduced-calorie mayonnaise and nonfat yogurt or "light" sour cream in this recipe.

12 servings

24	red-skinned potatoes, about 2 inches in diameter, quartered
1	cup mayonnaise
¼	cup minced fresh parsley
¼	teaspoon freshly ground pepper
3	cups plain yogurt or sour cream
¾	pound whitefish or salmon freshwater caviar
	Olive oil for brushing grill rack

Soak 12 bamboo skewers in cold water for 15 minutes; drain.

Parboil potatoes until just about tender. Drain and set aside until cool enough to handle. Thread potatoes on the drained skewers and let them cool completely.

Meanwhile light the coals, and then mix mayonnaise, parsley, and pepper in a bowl. Brush skewered potatoes with mayonnaise mixture.

When the coals are hot, place the grill rack, brushed with oil, about 4 to 6 inches from the heat source. Set the potato kabobs on the rack. Cook for about 8 to 10 minutes, turning the skewers every 2 to 3 minutes. When done, potatoes will be browned and all traces of mayonnaise will be gone.

Set one kabob on each plate. Add a large dollop of yogurt or sour cream and top it with caviar. Serve while potatoes are hot.

Antipasto Platter

6 to 8 servings

3	small Oriental white or purple eggplants, cut in half lengthwise
	Salt
2	large red bell peppers, seeded and quartered
1	medium-sized red onion, sliced
1	medium-sized yellow summer squash, cut into ½-inch slices
2	medium-sized tomatoes, cut into ½-inch slices
½	cup olive oil
3	tablespoons red wine vinegar
1	teaspoon dried basil
½	teaspoon dried oregano
¼	teaspoon salt
¼	teaspoon freshly ground pepper
1	cup dried oregano, soaked in cold water for 10 minutes and drained, as an aromatic
1	2-ounce jar pimientos, drained
1	15-ounce can chick-peas, drained
½	cup pimiento-stuffed green olives

Sprinkle cut side of eggplants with salt and let stand on paper towels, cut side down, for 30 minutes to drain. Rinse off salt and pat dry. Arrange eggplant, bell pepper, onion, squash, and tomatoes on a platter.

Mix together oil, vinegar, basil, ½ teaspoon oregano, salt, and pepper. Brush vegetables with dressing.

When the coals are hot, sprinkle them with 1 cup oregano. Set vegetables on grill rack about 4 to 6 inches from heat source. Grill eggplant, cut side down, for about 4 minutes, turn over, and continue grilling until soft. At the same time, grill the other vegetables on both sides until hot and slightly charred. Transfer all vegetables to a platter.

Sprinkle with chick-peas, pimientos, and olives. Serve hot or at room temperature. Good served with Italian bread or sesame bread sticks.

Antipasto Kabobs

8 servings

8	slices salami, casing removed
8	small mild pickled peppers, drained
2	small zucchini, quartered crosswise
16	pitted black olives
16	cherry tomatoes, washed and drained
⅓	cup olive oil
2	tablespoons freshly squeezed lemon juice
1	tablespoon balsamic vinegar
¼	teaspoon dried oregano
1	clove garlic, minced
¼	teaspoon salt
¼	teaspoon freshly ground white pepper

Soak eight bamboo skewers in cold water for 15 minutes; drain. Wrap a slice of salami around a small pepper and thread on a skewer. Thread on a piece of zucchini, an olive, a tomato, then another olive and another tomato. Repeat with remaining skewers and set kabobs aside.

Light the coals, and then mix remaining ingredients. Brush kabobs with this Italian dressing.

When the coals are hot, set kabobs on a grill rack about 4 to 6 inches from heat source. Grill kabobs for 3 to 4 minutes, turning once or twice as needed. Food should be hot and beginning to char.

Transfer kabobs to a serving dish and serve hot.

Grilled Eggplant Salad

8 servings

2	eggplants, about 7 inches long, cut in half lengthwise
	Olive oil for brushing eggplant and grill rack
2	tablespoons freshly squeezed lemon juice
1	medium-sized onion, minced
2	tablespoons olive oil
2	medium-sized tomatoes, peeled, seeded, and chopped
½	teaspoon salt
4	cloves garlic, minced
¾	teaspoon dried oregano
½	teaspoon ground cumin
⅓	cup chopped pimiento-stuffed green olives, ¼ cup brine reserved
½	cup chopped celery

Prepare the grill, and when the coals are hot, brush cut side of eggplant halves with oil. Set on grill rack, brushed with oil, about 4 to 6 inches from heat source. Grill until flesh is soft, about 5 to 7 minutes; eggplant will char. Brush eggplant with oil, turn over, and continue grilling until tender, about 5 to 7 minutes longer. Cool eggplant.

Scoop pulp from eggplant skins and spoon into a bowl. Mix in lemon juice, onion, 2 tablespoons oil, and tomatoes. Season with remaining ingredients. Cover lightly and refrigerate until ready to serve.

At serving time, toss eggplant salad and serve. Good with crudités, crackers, or toast points.

Pasta with Grilled Red Pepper Strips

This pasta dish is delicious served hot or cold.

8 servings

3	medium-sized red bell peppers
4	large cloves garlic, unpeeled
	Olive oil for brushing garlic
1	pound fettuccine
¼	cup olive oil
1	teaspoon cider vinegar
2	tablespoons margarine or butter, at room temperature
¼	teaspoon salt
¼	teaspoon freshly ground pepper
½	teaspoon dried oregano
3	tablespoons minced fresh parsley
¼	cup (or to taste) freshly grated Parmesan cheese

Prepare the grill, and when the coals are hot, set peppers on grill rack set 4 to 6 inches from heat source. Turn them as they become charred on each side. At the same time, brush garlic cloves with oil and set on rack. Turn garlic every 5 minutes until soft—about 12 to 15 minutes.

When peppers are charred all over, place in a self-sealing plastic bag and seal. Let peppers stand for 8 to 10 minutes. Remove peppers from bag and rub off the skin; it should slip off easily. Seed peppers and cut into thin strips; set aside.

When garlic is soft, remove cloves from grill and squeeze out soft garlic. Set aside.

While peppers and garlic are grilling, bring a large pot of salted water to a boil, add fettuccine, and cook for the time suggested on package, until al dente. Drain.

To assemble dish, place fettuccine in a warmed bowl. Toss pasta with garlic, oil, vinegar, margarine, salt, pepper, oregano, and parsley. If you want to serve this dish cold, chill it at this point.

Divide the pasta (either hot or cold) among eight individual plates. Set pepper strips over pasta and sprinkle with cheese.

Smoked Corn and Pepper Relish

This relish is good served with small biscuits.

8 servings

3	cups hickory chips, soaked in cold water for 1 hour and drained
4	ears corn, husks and silk removed
	Melted margarine or butter for brushing corn
6	strips bacon, cooked and crumbled
2	medium-sized green bell peppers, seeded and chopped
4	scallions, minced
¼	cup chopped cilantro
8	lettuce leaves for garnish

Prepare smoker according to manufacturer's directions. When coals are hot, sprinkle with drained wood. Using pot holders, set water pan, about two-thirds full of hot water, in place.

Brush corn with melted margarine and set on bottom rack. Cover smoker and cook for 15 minutes. Remove kernels from cobs with a small sharp knife. Place kernels in a bowl. Mix in crumbled bacon, peppers, scallions, and cilantro. Toss ingredients.

Serve relish at room temperature on a lettuce leaf on individual plates or on a layer of lettuce in a serving bowl.

Grilled Marinated Mushrooms

The combination of marinating and grilling gives these mushrooms a deep, complex flavor.

8 servings

½   cup cider vinegar
1   cup olive oil
3   cloves garlic, minced
2   tablespoons minced fresh parsley
½   teaspoon dried oregano
¼   teaspoon dried sage
¼   teaspoon salt
¼   teaspoon dried hot red pepper flakes
1   medium-sized red onion, sliced
2   pounds large mushrooms, stems trimmed
    Canola oil for brushing grill rack

In a glass or ceramic bowl, mix together vinegar, oil, garlic, parsley, oregano, sage, salt, pepper, and onion rings. Clean mushrooms with a damp paper towel. Toss mushrooms with marinade. Cover tightly and refrigerate for 24 hours, tossing mushrooms occasionally.

Prepare the grill, and when the coals are hot, place grill rack, brushed with oil, about 4 to 6 inches from heat source. Drain mushrooms and set mushrooms and onions on grill rack. Grill for about 3 minutes, turning once. Mushrooms will begin to brown and will be hot.

Transfer vegetables to a serving dish. Serve with toothpicks, cherry tomatoes, and crackers.

Grilled Marinated Leeks and Mushrooms

Since leeks tend to be sandy, they require a particularly diligent washing. Here's a recipe that's worth that extra effort.

8 servings

4	large leeks, cut in half lengthwise
2	pounds large white mushrooms, stems trimmed
2	cloves garlic, minced
1	cup olive oil or canola oil
¼	cup freshly squeezed lemon juice
¼	cup red wine vinegar
1	medium-sized onion, chopped
¼	cup minced fresh parsley
¾	teaspoon dried basil
½	teaspoon dried tarragon
½	teaspoon salt
¼	teaspoon freshly ground white pepper
	Canola oil for brushing grill rack
½	cup dried basil, soaked in water for 10 minutes and drained, as an aromatic

Poach leeks by adding them to a pan of boiling salted water. Reduce heat to simmer and continue cooking for 5 minutes. Leeks will be tender. Remove leeks with a slotted spoon. Drain and cool.

Meanwhile, clean mushrooms with a damp paper towel. Arrange mushrooms in a glass serving bowl. Toss with garlic, oil, lemon juice, vinegar, onion, parsley, basil, tarragon, salt, and pepper. Add leeks. Cover bowl lightly with plastic wrap and marinate in refrigerator for 24 hours, tossing occasionally.

Prepare the grill, and when the coals are hot, place grill rack, brushed with oil, about 4 to 6 inches from heat source. Sprinkle basil over hot coals. Drain leeks and mushrooms and set on rack. Grill for 3 to 4 minutes or until done, turning after 2 minutes. Vegetables should be hot and just beginning to brown. Remove vegetables from grill and set on individual plates. Serve hot.

Grilled Pumpkin Ravioli with Yogurt Curry Sauce

8 servings

Filling

2	tablespoons margarine or butter
¼	cup chopped mushrooms
1	rib celery, minced
1	small onion, minced
¼	teaspoon salt
1	cup pumpkin puree
¼	teaspoon ground cinnamon

Dough

2	cups all-purpose flour
¼	teaspoon salt
3	eggs
2	egg whites
2 to 3	tablespoons olive oil or canola oil

Yogurt Curry Sauce

2	cups plain nonfat yogurt
3	scallions, minced
1	teaspoon curry powder
¼	teaspoon ground cumin
2	quarts water
	Salt
	Canola oil to brush ravioli and grill rack

For filling, melt margarine in a saucepan over medium heat. Add mushrooms, celery, and onion. Sprinkle with salt and sauté for 5 minutes, stirring occasionally. Stir in pumpkin puree and cinnamon. Continue simmering for 3 minutes. Remove from heat and cool.

For dough, mix flour and salt in a deep mixing bowl or a food processor fitted with steel blade. Add eggs and egg whites. Stir in oil. Dough will be slightly sticky to the touch. Gather dough into a ball. Divide dough in half. Use a pasta machine for best results. Roll out half of the dough about $1/_8$ inch thick on a lightly floured surface.

Place $1/2$ teaspoon of filling every $2\frac{1}{2}$ inches along sheet of dough. Roll out remaining dough and place on top of ravioli. Press down edges. Cut into $2\frac{1}{2}$-inch squares or use a ravioli form. Sprinkle lightly with flour to prevent sticking.

For sauce, spoon yogurt into a bowl. Mix in scallions, curry powder, and cumin. Cover and refrigerate until needed.

Bring 2 quarts salted water to a boil in a saucepan. Slide in ravioli. Cook for 2 to 3 minutes or until just tender. Drain.

Prepare the grill, and when the coals are hot, place grill rack, brushed with oil, about 4 to 6 inches from heat source. Set ravioli on grill rack and cook for about 2 to 3 minutes, turning once. Ravioli will brown slightly and be hot.

Divide ravioli among eight individual plates. Stir sauce and spoon a dollop of it into the middle of each dish. Serve immediately.

White Polenta with Rosemary

White cornmeal instead of the traditional yellow is used for this polenta, which is flavored with fresh rosemary.

8 to 10 servings

3	tablespoons margarine or butter
1	small red onion, minced
1	quart water
1	cup white cornmeal
2	teaspoons chopped fresh rosemary
½	teaspoon salt
¼	teaspoon freshly ground white pepper
¼	teaspoon dried oregano
3	tablespoons margarine or butter, melted
	Canola oil for brushing grill rack
	Freshly grated Romano or Parmesan cheese

Heat 3 tablespoons margarine in a medium saucepan over medium heat. Add onion and sauté for 4 minutes, stirring occasionally. Stir in water and bring to a boil. Slowly whisk in cornmeal. Continue whisking to prevent lumps from forming. Stir in rosemary, salt, pepper, and oregano. Continue cooking until mixture thickens, about 10 to 12 minutes.

Pour polenta into an oiled 9-inch round cake pan. Cool, then refrigerate for 20 to 30 minutes or until polenta is firm. The polenta can be prepared up to this point the day before serving.

Cut polenta into pie-shaped wedges and brush both sides with melted margarine.

Prepare the grill, and when the coals are hot, place grill rack about 4 to 6 inches from heat source. Place polenta on grill rack and cook for 4 minutes, turning once. Polenta will brown lightly and be hot.

Transfer polenta to a serving dish. Sprinkle with cheese and serve hot.

Mushroom Wontons
with Jalapeño Salsa

Wonton wrappers are available at most large supermarkets and at Oriental food markets.

Wear rubber gloves when handling jalapeños and don't touch your eyes.

8 servings

Salsa

1	large green bell pepper
1 to 3	(to taste) jalapeño peppers, cut in half lengthwise and seeded
3	medium-sized tomatoes, peeled, seeded, and chopped
½	cup chopped cilantro
3	tablespoons freshly squeezed lemon juice
2	cloves garlic, minced
½	teaspoon chili powder
½	teaspoon salt
¼	teaspoon dried thyme

Wontons

¼	cup margarine or butter
3	shallots, minced
¾	pound mushrooms, chopped
½	cup half-and-half
¼	teaspoon dried marjoram
¼	teaspoon dried basil
¼	teaspoon salt
¼	teaspoon freshly ground pepper
1	1-pound package wonton wrappers
1	egg white
	All-purpose flour to sprinkle on cookie sheet
2	quarts water
	Canola oil for brushing grill rack and wontons

Prepare the grill, and when the coals are hot, place bell pepper for salsa on grill rack. Turn pepper as it becomes charred on each side. When it is charred all over, place pepper in a self-sealing plastic bag and seal. Let stand for 8 to 10 minutes. Remove pepper from bag and rub off skin; it should slip off easily. Seed and chop pepper and put into a bowl.

Grill the jalapeño pepper on a grill rack for 1 minute on each side; cut open the pepper, and discard seeds. Chop it and add to bell pepper. Mix in remaining salsa ingredients. Cover salsa and refrigerate for 1 hour.

For wontons, melt margarine in a large frying pan. Add shallots and mushrooms and sauté over low heat for about 6 minutes or until mushrooms are cooked and almost dry, stirring occasionally.

Stir in half-and-half and continue cooking until mixture is thick. Season with marjoram, basil, salt, and pepper. Taste and adjust seasonings. Cool. The wonton filling can be made up to several hours ahead of time and refrigerated.

To assemble place 2 to 3 teaspoons of filling into the center of the wrapper. Brush outside edge of the wrapper with slightly beaten egg white. To seal it shut, fold wrapper in half-envelope style and press along seam, sealing wrapper shut. Place filled wontons on lightly floured cookie sheet.

Bring water to a boil in a medium saucepan. Slide wontons into boiling water. Cook for 2 minutes or until wontons are tender. Remove wontons with a slotted spoon and place on a dish in a single layer. Cover and refrigerate until ready to grill. You can prepare the wontons up to 2 hours ahead of time.

Prepare the grill, and when the coals are hot, place grill rack, brushed with oil, about 4 to 6 inches from heat source. Brush wontons lightly with oil and place on grill rack. Cook for 2 minutes, turning once. Wontons will begin to color and will be hot. Toss salsa and taste to adjust seasoning. Serve with hot wontons.

Artichoke Bottoms
with Bay Scallops

8 servings

¾ pound bay scallops, washed
1   cup fresh fine bread crumbs
3   tablespoons minced fresh parsley
½   teaspoon dried tarragon
¼   cup minced celery
2   cloves garlic, minced
2   14-ounce cans artichoke bottoms, drained
    Canola oil for brushing grill rack

Mix scallops, bread crumbs, parsley, tarragon, celery, and garlic in a bowl. Gently mound filling into artichoke bottoms.

Prepare the grill, and when the coals are hot, set artichokes on a grill rack, brushed with oil, about 4 to 6 inches from the heat source. Cover grill and cook stuffed artichokes for about 3 minutes or until scallops are opaque.

Using a long-handled spatula, transfer artichoke bottoms to a serving dish and serve hot.

Stuffed Sweet Peppers

Sweet peppers imported from Holland are about 3 to 4 inches long and 1½ inches wide. They come in orange, purple, and yellow.

8 servings

¼	pound bay scallops, washed
½	pound skinless salmon fillet, cut into small pieces
½	cup fresh fine bread crumbs
3	tablespoons minced fresh parsley
½	teaspoon dried tarragon
2	cloves garlic, minced
8	assorted select Holland peppers, cut in half and seeds removed
	Canola oil for brushing grill rack
	Fresh parsley sprigs for garnish

Mix together scallops, salmon, bread crumbs, parsley, tarragon, and garlic. Stuff peppers with filling and refrigerate peppers until coals are hot.

Prepare the grill, and when the coals are hot, set the grill rack, brushed with oil, about 4 to 6 inches from heat source. Cook stuffed peppers for about 2 minutes on each side or until filling is cooked.

Using a long-handled spatula, transfer peppers to a serving dish and serve hot, garnished with parsley.

Stuffed Mushrooms

8 servings

3	tablespoons olive oil
24	medium-large mushrooms, stems removed and chopped
2	large shallots, minced
½	cup chopped walnuts
½	cup minced celery
¾	cup fresh fine whole-wheat bread crumbs
½	teaspoon dried tarragon
¼	teaspoon salt
¼	cup minced fresh parsley
	Olive oil for brushing mushrooms and grill rack

Heat oil in a frying pan. Add mushroom stems and shallots and sauté over medium heat for 3 minutes, stirring occasionally.

Mix in walnuts, celery, bread crumbs, tarragon, salt, and parsley. Clean mushrooms with a damp paper towel. Gently mound stuffing into mushroom caps. Brush bottom of mushrooms with oil.

Prepare the grill, and when the coals are hot, place grill rack, brushed with oil, about 4 to 6 inches from heat source. Set mushrooms on rack, cover grill, and cook for 2 to 3 minutes or until mushrooms are firm to the touch (not mushy).

Transfer mushrooms to a tray and serve hot.

POULTRY

Zucchini Stuffed with Chicken Curry

Since this dish doesn't use the flesh from the zucchini, you might want to use it for soup.

8 servings

3	tablespoons canola oil
1	small onion, minced
2	cloves garlic, minced
1	rib celery, minced
2	tablespoons chopped fresh parsley
1	teaspoon curry powder
½	teaspoon ground cumin
¼	teaspoon salt
¼	teaspoon freshly ground pepper
1	boneless, skinless chicken breast, ground
8	small to medium zucchini, cut in half lengthwise, flesh scooped out and discarded

Heat oil in a frying pan. Add onion, garlic, and celery and sauté over medium heat for 4 minutes, stirring occasionally. Stir in parsley, curry powder, cumin, salt, and pepper. Mix in ground chicken and stir to combine. Remove from heat and cool.

Stuff zucchini shells with chicken mixture, mounding and firming the filling. Pat filling to keep it in place. Refrigerate the zucchini shells until the coals are ready.

Prepare the grill, and when the coals are hot, place stuffed zucchini on grill rack, brushed with oil. Grill, covered, for about 6 minutes, until chicken is cooked and filling is firm to the touch.

Chicken Wings with Sesame Seed Sauce

You can save the tips removed from the chicken wings for stock. Tahini, a sesame seed paste, is available at large supermarkets, health food stores, and Middle Eastern food markets.

8 servings

Sesame Seed Sauce

¾	cup tahini
3	cloves garlic, peeled
2	tablespoons freshly squeezed lemon juice
¾	cup water
1	teaspoon sugar
¼	cup fresh mint leaves

Brushing Sauce

½	cup peanut oil or canola oil
¼	cup red wine vinegar
¼	cup minced cilantro
¼	teaspoon freshly ground pepper

24	chicken wings, disjointed and tips removed
1	cup pitted black olives for garnish

Put all sesame seed sauce ingredients in a food processor fitted with a steel blade and puree. Spoon sauce into a serving dish. Cover and refrigerate until serving time.

For brushing sauce, stir together oil, vinegar, cilantro, and pepper. Brush chicken wings liberally with sauce.

Prepare the grill, and when the coals are hot, set chicken wings on a grill rack about 4 to 6 inches from heat source. Cook chicken wings for about 6 to 8 minutes, turning once or twice as necessary. Wings will char and be cooked through.

When wings are almost ready, remove sesame seed sauce from refrigerator, stir, and add more water, a tablespoon at a time, until sauce is desired thickness for pouring.

Transfer wings to a plate and serve hot with sauce drizzled over them.

Chicken Saté with Peanut/Coconut Sauce

Homemade peanut butter is best for the Peanut/Coconut Sauce.

8 servings

1¼	pounds boneless, skinless chicken breast
¾	cup canned coconut milk
1½	teaspoons curry powder
2	teaspoons sugar
¼	teaspoon ground ginger
2	scallions, minced

Peanut/Coconut Sauce

1¼	cups chunky peanut butter
¾	cup canned coconut milk
1	tablespoon sugar
¼	teaspoon salt
3	tablespoons hot water
¼	teaspoon garlic powder
1	cup chopped cilantro for garnish
	Canola oil for brushing grill rack

Soak 16 bamboo skewers in cold water for 15 minutes; drain.

Place each piece of chicken between two sheets of waxed paper and pound thin. Cut chicken into 1-inch strips.

Mix ¾ cup coconut milk, curry powder, 2 teaspoons sugar, ginger, and scallions in a bowl. Pour marinade into a large self-sealing plastic bag. Add chicken and seal bag securely. Turn bag several times so that chicken is covered by marinade. Set bag of chicken in a shallow dish and refrigerate for 3 to 4 hours, turning the bag two or three times.

While chicken is marinating, prepare sauce. In a small saucepan, stir together peanut butter, ¾ cup coconut milk, 1 tablespoon sugar, salt, hot water, and garlic powder. Cook over low heat until sauce is warm, stirring almost constantly.

Prepare the grill, and when the coals are hot, drain chicken and thread on skewers. Place saté on grill rack, brushed with oil, about 4 to 6 inches from heat source. Cook for 3 to 4 minutes, turning once. Chicken is done when its juices run clear when meat is pierced with a fork. Do not overcook chicken, or it will become tough. Meanwhile, reheat sauce if necessary.

To serve, place chicken saté on a plate, sprinkle with cilantro, and pass the sauce.

Grilled Chicken Fingers
with Double Mustard Sauce

8 servings

Tarragon Marinade

1	cup olive oil or canola oil
½	cup cider vinegar
1	tablespoon minced fresh parsley
½	teaspoon dried tarragon
¼	teaspoon freshly ground pepper
2	bay leaves

1½   pounds boneless, skinless chicken breasts, sliced into finger-shaped pieces ½ inch by 3 to 4 inches

Double Mustard Sauce

1	cup mayonnaise
1	tablespoon stone-ground mustard
1	teaspoon dry mustard
1	teaspoon drained capers
¼	teaspoon freshly ground pepper
1	scallion, minced

For marinade, mix together oil, vinegar, parsley, tarragon, pepper, and bay leaves. Divide chicken between two large self-sealing plastic bags. Add marinade and seal bags securely. Turn bags several times so that all chicken pieces are coated with marinade. Set bags in a bowl and marinate in refrigerator for 3 to 4 hours, turning occasionally.

While chicken is marinating, prepare sauce. Spoon mayonnaise into a small bowl. Mix in remaining ingredients. Cover and refrigerate.

Prepare the grill, and when the coals are hot, drain chicken and discard marinade. Set chicken on grill rack about 4 to 6 inches from heat source. Remove the sauce from the refrigerator so it can warm to room temperature. Cook chicken for 6 to 8 minutes, turning once or twice, as necessary. Chicken will char, and juices will run clear when meat is pierced with a fork. Do not overcook.

Blackened Chicken Nuggets with Grilled Kiwifruit

8 servings

Balsamic Marinade

1	cup canola oil
¼	cup balsamic vinegar
½	cup beer
1	teaspoon dried rosemary

2	pounds boneless, skinless chicken breasts

Blackening Spices

½	teaspoon salt
2	tablespoons garlic powder
¼	teaspoon freshly ground pepper
2	teaspoons dried thyme
2	teaspoons dried oregano
2	tablespoons paprika
1¼	tablespoons minced dried onion

	Canola oil for brushing grill rack and kiwifruits
4	kiwifruits, peeled and cut in half

For marinade, mix oil, vinegar, beer, and rosemary in a bowl. Pour into two large self-sealing plastic bags. Add chicken breasts and seal securely. Turn bag several times so that chicken is coated with marinade. Marinate in refrigerator for 3 to 4 hours, turning occasionally.

Combine blackening spices in a small bowl. Drain chicken and sprinkle spices over both sides. Chicken can remain in refrigerator with spices or until coals are ready.

Prepare the grill, and when the coals are hot, place chicken on grill rack, brushed with oil, about 4 to 6 inches from heat source. Cook chicken for 6 to 8 minutes, turning once or twice as necessary. Chicken will char, and juices will run clear when meat is pierced with a fork. While chicken is grilling, brush kiwifruit with oil and set on grill rack. Cook for about 2 minutes, turning once.

Transfer chicken to cutting board and cut into 1-inch chunks. Serve chicken hot or warm with toothpicks and grilled kiwifruit.

Stuffed Oriental Chicken Wings

To bone chicken wings, bone just the larger side and reserve the wing for chicken stock. Use a small sharp knife. Carefully cut away at the cartilage as you push down on the meat. When you get to the bottom of the wing, twist off the bone. This process speeds up with practice. You can bone the chicken wings ahead of time and freeze them. Defrost when you are ready to marinate. You can use the discarded wing tips for chicken stock.

8 servings

Mustard Marinade

1½	tablespoons stone-ground mustard
1	cup olive oil or canola oil
4	cloves garlic, minced
½	cup dry white wine
2	bay leaves
2	tablespoons minced fresh parsley
32	chicken wings, disjointed, larger part boned, wing tips reserved for stock

Stuffing

2	tablespoons peanut oil or canola oil
2	cloves garlic, minced
½	teaspoon grated fresh gingerroot
3	scallions, minced
1	cup minced celery
½	cup grated carrot
1	cup chopped water chestnuts
2	tablespoons light soy sauce
¼	teaspoon salt
¼	teaspoon freshly ground pepper

Canola oil for brushing grill rack

For marinade, stir mustard into oil. Blend in garlic, wine, bay leaves, and parsley. Divide marinade between two large self-sealing plastic bags. Add chicken wings and seal bags securely. Turn bags several times so that all sides of wings are touched by marinade. Set bags on a flat dish and refrigerate for 3 to 4 hours.

Meanwhile, prepare stuffing. Heat oil in a wok or frying pan. Add garlic, gingerroot, and scallions and sauté over low heat for about 2 minutes, stirring often until scallions are tender. Stir in celery, carrots, and water chestnuts. Cook over medium-high heat, stirring often, until vegetables are tender, about 3 to 5 minutes. Stir in soy sauce, salt, and pepper. Remove vegetables from heat. Drain chicken wings from marinade. Using a small spoon, stuff chicken wings.

Prepare the grill, and when the coals are hot, place wings on a grill rack, brushed with oil, about 4 to 6 inches from heat source. Cook for 6 to 8 minutes, turning once or twice as necessary. Wings will char and be cooked through. (You can remove one wing and cut into it to be sure it's done.)

Transfer wings to a plate and serve hot. You might want to serve with Oriental mustard and plum sauce for dipping.

Bourbon Turkey Dogs

You can also use cocktail franks, left whole.

8 servings

1	cup bourbon
¾	cup catsup
¼	cup homemade or canned tomato sauce (see Index for Rosemary/Basil Sauce)
¾	cup firmly packed light brown sugar
1	clove garlic, minced
2	pounds turkey hot dogs, cut into 1-inch pieces

Mix bourbon, catsup, tomato sauce, scallions, brown sugar, and garlic in a saucepan. Bring mixture to a boil over medium heat. Reduce heat to a simmer and continue cooking for 5 minutes, stirring occasionally. Remove sauce from heat. Add hot dog pieces and let stand for 1 hour.

Prepare the grill, and when the coals are hot, drain hot dogs and reserve sauce. Set hot dogs on grill rack about 4 to 6 inches from heat source. Cook for about 5 to 6 minutes, rotating hot dogs as they char. The meat will be cooked through and browned.

Reheat reserved sauce, place hot dogs in a deep bowl, and mix in sauce. Serve with toothpicks, scallion spears, and carrot sticks.

Petit Turkey Sausage

Every Mother's Day, my husband plants an herb garden for me. We raise the herbs used frequently in cooking—parsley, tarragon, basil, rosemary, sage, dill, and chives. These fresh herbs make a huge difference in the taste of food. I use tarragon and mint sticks as kabobs and herbs as aromatics on the grill. Try raising some herbs. Even a window box will do nicely.

8 servings

1¼	pounds ground turkey
3	scallions, minced
¾	teaspoon dried sage
½	teaspoon dried marjoram
1	egg white, slightly beaten
¼	cup minced fresh parsley
¼	teaspoon salt
¼	teaspoon freshly ground white pepper
	Fresh sage leaves, if available
	Canola oil for brushing grill rack

Crumble turkey into a bowl. Mix in scallions, sage, marjoram, egg white, parsley, salt, and pepper. Shape turkey mixture into 2-inch sausages. (If you have mint stems at hand, shape the turkey mixture around the stems as skewers. Wrap edges of mint sticks with aluminum foil.) Put a sage leaf, if available, on each sausage or on some of them.

Prepare the grill, and when the coals are hot, place turkey sausages on grill rack, brushed with oil, about 4 to 6 inches from heat source. Cook sausages for about 2 minutes on each side. Turkey sausage will brown slightly and turn a whitish color. Transfer sausage to a serving dish. Serve hot with small pickles and cocktail rye bread.

Grilled Marinated Turkey Club with Jalapeño Mayonnaise

This recipe is from Don Hysko of Peoples Coal, Rhode Island. Don is a master of the art of grilling. Use green applewood on the coals for extra flavor.

Be sure to wear rubber gloves when handling jalapeños and be careful not to touch your eyes.

4 servings

Marinade

1	cup olive oil
⅓	cup freshly squeezed lemon juice
½	cup mixed chopped fresh parsley, rosemary, thyme, and basil

Sandwiches

2	boneless turkey breast slices, ½ inch thick and cut in half (4 pieces)
8	slices coarse-grain bread, sliced ½ inch thick
8	strips smoked or country-style bacon, cooked
4	medium-sized ripe tomatoes, sliced ¼ inch thick and seeded
1	head red leaf lettuce or curly leaf lettuce, separated into leaves

Jalapeño Mayonnaise

2	fresh jalapeño peppers
1	cup mayonnaise
2	tablespoons chopped drained capers
	Juice of 1 lemon
1	tablespoon Worcestershire sauce
	Salt and freshly ground pepper to taste

For marinade, in a shallow dish, combine oil and lemon juice until well mixed; whisk in herbs. Add turkey and cover with plastic wrap or transfer turkey and marinade to self-sealing plastic bags. Marinate in refrigerator for several hours.

Prepare the grill, and when the coals are hot, drain turkey and place on a grill rack 4 to 6 inches from heat source. Grill for 3 to 4 minutes, turning once, or until meat is no longer pink.

Transfer to a warm platter. Grill bread on both sides. Remove, and set aside.

For mayonnaise, toast peppers on grill until tender, about 1 minute on each side. Split peppers, remove seeds and veins; chop fine. In a bowl, mix peppers with remaining mayonnaise ingredients.

To assemble sandwiches, spread one side of each slice of bread with mayonnaise. Place grilled turkey on bread. Top each with two strips of bacon, tomatoes, and lettuce. Stack two sandwiches together and cap with remaining slice of bread. To serve, cut into quarters and lay, crust down, on a platter.

SEAFOOD

Stuffed Smelts

8 servings

2	2-ounce cans flat anchovy fillets, drained
24	smelts, cleaned and heads discarded
1	cup fresh fine bread crumbs
2	tablespoons minced fresh parsley
½	teaspoon dried oregano
¼	teaspoon dried marjoram
8	scallions, cleaned
	Olive oil or canola oil for brushing grill rack and scallions
	Tomato wedges for garnish

Place one anchovy fillet inside each smelt.

Pour bread crumbs into a flat dish. Mix in parsley, oregano, and marjoram. Roll smelts in seasoned bread crumbs. Refrigerate smelts until coals are ready.

Prepare the grill, and when the coals are hot, place smelts on grill rack, brushed with oil, about 4 to 6 inches from heat source. Grill smelts for 5 minutes, turning once. The smelts will brown and be cooked through. Brush scallions with oil and set on rack. Grill for about 3 minutes, turning once. Scallions will begin to color.

Arrange smelts decoratively on a serving dish with the grilled scallions and tomato wedges.

Shrimp on a Skewer

This shrimp is good served with pita bread warmed on the grill.

8 servings

Lemon Marinade

½   cup olive oil or canola oil
     Juice of 1 large lemon or lime
½   teaspoon grated lemon zest
3   cloves garlic, minced
3   bay leaves
2   tablespoons minced fresh parsley
1   pound (about 24) extra-large shrimp, peeled, deveined, tails left intact
8   large bay leaves
¼   cup dried oregano, soaked in cold water for 10 minutes and drained, as an aromatic
½   pound feta cheese, crumbled

Soak eight bamboo skewers in cold water for 15 minutes; drain. For marinade, combine oil, juice, lemon zest, garlic, 3 bay leaves, and parsley in a bowl. Pour mixture into a large self-sealing plastic bag. Add shrimp and seal bag securely. Turn bag over so that the surface of all the shrimp will be touched by marinade. Marinate the shrimp for 3 to 4 hours in the refrigerator, turning bag once or twice.

Prepare the grill, and when the coals are hot, drain shrimp, discarding marinade. Thread shrimp on skewers, ending with a large bay leaf. Place kabobs on grill rack about 4 to 6 inches from heat source. Sprinkle oregano over hot coals for an aromatic effect. Cook shrimp for 4 to 6 minutes or until done, turning once. Shrimp are cooked when they turn a white-pink color. Overcooked shrimp become tough and rubbery.

To serve, place shrimp on individual plates and sprinkle with crumbled feta cheese. Remind guests to discard bay leaf.

Stuffed Clams

        2   tablespoons canola oil
        3   scallions, minced
        2   cloves garlic, minced
        1   6½-ounce can minced clams, drained and liquid reserved
        1   cup fresh whole-wheat bread crumbs
        ¼   teaspoon dried oregano
        ¼   teaspoon dried basil
        ¼   teaspoon salt
        ¼   teaspoon freshly ground pepper
       18   clam shells, cleaned, or clam shell ramekins
        ¼   cup freshly grated Parmesan cheese, plus extra if desired

Heat oil in a frying pan. Add scallions and garlic and sauté over medium heat for 3 to 4 minutes, until scallions are tender, stirring occasionally. Stir in clams, bread crumbs, oregano, basil, salt, and pepper. Add only enough clam liquid to make mixture slightly moist, about 1 tablespoon.

Spoon mixture into clam shells. Sprinkle with Parmesan cheese. Refrigerate clam shells until coals are ready.

Prepare the grill, and when the coals are hot, set stuffed clam shells on grill rack about 4 to 6 inches from heat source. Cover grill and cook for 5 minutes. Stuffing will be hot when done.

Remove stuffed clams and set on individual small plates or on a platter to serve from a buffet. You may want to pass extra Parmesan cheese at the table. Serve hot.

Smoked Tuna with Raspberry Vinegar Dressing

8 servings

8	5-ounce tuna steaks
3	cups mesquite chips or other wood, such as apple, plum, or cherry, soaked in cold water for 1 hour and drained
	Olive oil or canola oil for brushing tuna
1	orange, sliced thin

Raspberry Vinegar Dressing

½	cup raspberry vinegar
¾	cup canola oil
3	shallots, minced
1	teaspoon chopped fresh mint
1	teaspoon sugar
¼	teaspoon salt
¼	teaspoon freshly ground pepper

Prepare smoker according to manufacturer's directions. When the coals are hot, sprinkle with drained mesquite chips. Using pot holders, set the water pan, about two-thirds full of hot water, in place.

Brush tuna with oil. Set orange slices on grill and place tuna on top. Cover smoker and cook tuna for about 45 minutes. Tuna is done when firm to the touch and easy to flake. Do not overcook.

Meanwhile, mix all dressing ingredients in a bowl. Stir before using.

Set tuna on a plate and let stand for 5 minutes, cut into thin slices, and put three slices on each plate. Stir sauce and drizzle over tuna. Serve hot.

Grilled Oysters with Basil Sauce

It is not necessary to shuck oysters before grilling them. They will open from the heat of the fire.

6 servings

Basil Sauce

¼ cup margarine, butter, or a combination, at room temperature, cut into 1-inch pieces
2 tablespoons minced fresh basil
¼ teaspoon garlic powder
¼ teaspoon ground ginger
½ cup minced fresh parsley

Oysters

3 pounds kosher salt
30 oysters in the shell, scrubbed under cold running water

For sauce, place margarine in a food processor fitted with steel blade. Add basil, garlic, ginger, and parsley. Process until all ingredients are combined. Spoon into a serving bowl. Cover and refrigerate until serving time. Let stand at room temperature for 10 minutes before serving.

Prepare the grill, and when the coals are hot, arrange salt evenly in two 9-inch baking pans. Set oysters on salt. Set pans on grill rack about 4 to 6 inches from heat source. If you have a small grill, you might have to grill one pan at a time. If so, refrigerate the second pan until the first batch of oysters is done. Cover grill and cook oysters only for 1 to 2 minutes, just until they open. You will hear a slight popping noise as the shells open.

Bring pans of oysters to the table and set on a trivet. Using tongs, place oysters on individual plates. Pass basil butter to spoon onto open oysters.

Sea Scallop and Artichoke Kabobs

Scallops and artichokes are a sensational combination.

6 servings

Garlic Marinade

½	cup olive oil or canola oil
3	tablespoons freshly squeezed lime juice
3	cloves garlic, minced
1	scallion, minced
¼	teaspoon freshly ground white pepper
¼	teaspoon dried oregano

Kabobs

18	sea scallops
12	canned artichoke hearts, drained
6	cherry tomatoes
6	pitted black olives
	Olive oil or canola oil for brushing grill rack

Soak six bamboo skewers in cold water for 15 minutes; drain.

Combine marinade ingredients in a bowl. Pour mixture into a large self-sealing plastic bag. Add scallops and seal bag securely. Turn bag over so that all scallops are soaked in marinade. Marinate scallops in refrigerator for 2 hours, turning bag once or twice.

Prepare the grill, and when the coals are hot, drain scallops, reserving marinade as a brushing sauce. Thread skewers, alternating scallops with artichokes and ending with a tomato and an olive. Place kabob on grill rack, brushed with oil, about 4 to 6 inches from heat source. Brush kabobs with reserved marinade. Grill for 3 to 4 minutes on each side or until scallops are opaque. Remove kabobs and set on individual plates. Serve hot.

Soft-Shell Crabs with Herbs

Soft-shell crabs are wonderful because the entire crab is edible. They are available from May to October, when the crabs molt and their shells are soft enough to eat. To clean a soft-shell crab, lay the crab on a cutting board and cut off the face portion. Lift the shell on either side of the back, scrape off the gills, and discard. Again, lift the shell and discard the sand receptacle under the mouth area. Wash and dry the crab. You can also ask the people at the fish market to clean the crabs for you. Most of them will be glad to oblige.

6 servings

Hazelnut Sauce

½	cup ground hazelnuts
1½	cups plain nonfat yogurt
¼	teaspoon dried tarragon
¼	teaspoon dried sage

Crabs

¼	cup margarine or butter
¼	teaspoon dried tarragon
¼	teaspoon dried sage
1	cup fine fresh bread crumbs
12	soft-shell crabs
	Canola or olive oil for grill rack

For sauce, stir hazelnuts into yogurt in a small bowl. Mix in tarragon and sage. Cover and refrigerate until grilling time, then bring sauce to room temperature while crabs cook.

For crabs, melt margarine and stir in tarragon and sage. Brush both sides of crabs with flavored margarine. Sprinkle crabs with bread crumbs.

Prepare the grill, and when the coals are hot, place the crabs on grill rack, brushed with oil, about 4 to 6 inches from heat source. Cook for about 6 minutes, turning once. The crabs will turn a reddish color when done.

Put two crabs on each individual plate. Stir sauce and spoon a dollop of it onto each plate. Serve hot.

Mussels with White Wine

8 servings

6 dozen small mussels, scrubbed and debearded
½ cup dry white wine
8 bay leaves
1 medium-sized onion, minced
2 cloves garlic, minced
½ teaspoon dried thyme

Prepare the grill, and while coals are heating, cut eight 12-inch-long sheets of heavy-duty aluminum foil. Place nine mussels in center of each sheet of foil. Lift up sides of foil to form a cup shape. Sprinkle mussels with wine. Add a bay leaf and some onion, garlic, and thyme. Twist each package closed securely.

When the coals are hot, put mussel packages directly on hot coals. Cook for 6 minutes, carefully turning each package once. Do not overcook mussels; cook them only until they are just opened. Remove one package to see if mussels are done. Discard any unopened mussels and remind guests to discard bay leaves.

Allow guests to open packages individually. Serve mussels hot with French bread warmed on the grill.

Salmon and Pineapple Kabobs

8 servings

Cinnamon Brushing Sauce

3	tablespoons melted margarine or butter
¼	teaspoon ground cinnamon
$1/_8$	teaspoon freshly grated nutmeg
1	tablespoon light brown sugar

Kabobs

1	pound salmon fillet, cut into ¾-inch cubes
1	8-ounce can pineapple chunks packed in water, drained
	Canola oil for brushing grill rack

Soak eight bamboo skewers in cold water for 15 minutes; drain.

For brushing sauce, mix together margarine, cinnamon, nutmeg, and brown sugar. Set aside.

Thread skewers, alternating salmon and pineapple, using two pieces of fish and two chunks of pineapple on each skewer. Brush kabobs with brushing sauce. Kabobs will marinate while coals heat.

Prepare the grill, and when coals are hot, place kabobs on grill rack, brushed with oil, about 4 to 6 inches from the heat source. Grill for about 6 minutes, turning once or twice. Fish will be opaque and will flake easily when prodded with tines of a fork.

Set one kabob on each dish.

Crab Cakes on the Grill
with Tartar Sauce

8 servings

Tartar Sauce

- 1 cup mayonnaise
- 2 teaspoons drained capers
- ¼ teaspoon salt
- 2 tablespoons minced fresh parsley
- 1½ tablespoons chopped drained sweet pickle

Crab Cakes

- 2 tablespoons margarine or butter
- 4 scallions, minced
- ¼ cup chopped red bell pepper
- 1 rib celery, minced
- 1 egg white, slightly beaten
- 1½ cups fresh bread crumbs
- 1 pound imitation king crab meat, flaked
- ½ teaspoon salt
- ¼ teaspoon freshly ground white pepper
- ¼ teaspoon ground thyme
- ¼ teaspoon cayenne pepper
- 3 tablespoons mayonnaise
- 2 tablespoons chopped fresh parsley

Melted margarine or butter for brushing grill rack

Put sauce ingredients into a bowl and mix well. Cover and refrigerate until needed.

For crab cakes, heat 2 tablespoons margarine in a wide skillet and add scallions, red pepper, and celery. Sauté over low heat for 4 to 5 minutes or until scallions are tender. Spoon vegetables into a mixing bowl. Add egg white and bread crumbs, mixing well. Stir in crabmeat, salt, pepper, thyme, and cayenne. Blend in mayonnaise and parsley.

Shape mixture into 16 small crab cakes. Arrange on a plate and refrigerate for at least 40 minutes before grilling. These crab cakes can be prepared early in the day and refrigerated.

Prepare the grill, and when the coals are hot, place crab cakes on grill rack, brushed with melted margarine, about 4 to 6 inches from heat source. Cook for 6 to 8 minutes, turning once or twice. You may want to brush cakes with melted margarine when you turn them. When done, cakes will be firm and browned on the outside and cooked and moist in the center.

To serve, place hot crab cakes on a platter. Stir tartar sauce and serve with crab cakes.

CHEESE

Cheddar, Melon, and Italian Sausage

8 servings

1½   pounds sweet sausage
½   pound cheddar cheese, cut into 16 pieces
24   1-inch chunks honeydew melon or cantaloupe
     Melted margarine or butter for brushing grill rack

Soak eight bamboo skewers in cold water for 15 minutes; drain.

Prepare the grill for the indirect method. When the coals are hot, pour hot water into the pan between the coals. Replace grill about 4 to 6 inches from heat source and set sausages on a grill rack. Cool sausages for 5 to 10 minutes, rotating every 2 minutes, until sausage is cooked through. Grill sausages until almost cooked. Remove sausages and cut each one into four pieces.

To assemble kabobs, thread skewers evenly with cheese, melon, and pieces of sausage. Brush grill rack with melted margarine and set in place. Grill kabobs for about 2 minutes, turning once. When done, the food should be warm; do not let the cheese melt. Set kabobs on a dish and let guests help themselves. You might want to serve the kabobs with cocktail dark rye bread.

Grilled Brie with Peach Chutney

Chutney makes a great gift. Prepare extra so you always have some on hand.

8 servings (about 3½ cups chutney)

Brie

1	pound Brie cheese
1	egg white, slightly beaten
¾	cup fresh bread crumbs
½	teaspoon dried sage

Chutney

1¼	pounds peaches, peeled, pits removed, chopped
1	cup cranberries, washed
1	cup granulated sugar
⅓	cup firmly packed dark brown sugar
⅓	cup dried black currants
1	medium-sized onion, minced
1	tablespoon minced candied ginger
¼	cup raisins
1	teaspoon ground cinnamon
½	teaspoon ground cloves
¼	teaspoon ground mace
¼	teaspoon ground allspice
¾	cup water

Melted margarine or butter for brushing grill rack

Using a potato peeler, cut off some of the thick areas of the Brie rind around the rim, top and bottom. Cut cheese into eight equal wedges.

Pour egg white into a shallow dish. Spread bread crumbs on another dish and mix in sage. Roll cheese in egg white and then dust with bread crumbs. Shake off extra bread crumbs. Place cheese on a plate and refrigerate until ready to grill.

For chutney, combine peaches with cranberries in a medium saucepan. Mix in remaining chutney ingredients. Simmer, uncovered, for 25 to 30 minutes, stirring occasionally. Transfer chutney to a bowl, cover, and refrigerate until needed. Chutney can be kept refrigerated for 1 week. You can remove the peach chutney from the refrigerator just after you light the coals and let it warm to room temperature or serve the chutney cold.

Prepare the grill, and when the coals are hot, place cheese on grill rack, brushed with margarine, about 4 to 6 inches from heat source. Grill cheese for about 3 minutes, turning once. Cheese should be warm and just runny.

To serve, place a wedge of cheese on a small plate with a dollop of peach chutney on the side.

Basil Brie Toast

Basil Brie Toast is adapted from a favorite recipe served at Froggy's Restaurant in Highwood, Illinois. Chef Thierry Le Feuvre has created a perfect savory toast. With great liberty, we have adapted it for the grill.

8 servings
Pesto Sauce

2	cups fresh basil leaves
½	cup pine nuts
3	cloves garlic, minced
¼	teaspoon salt
½	cup olive oil
⅓	cup freshly grated Parmesan cheese
8	slices white or whole-wheat bread, cut in half, crusts removed
¾	pound Brie cheese, sliced thin, thick parts of rind trimmed off
	Melted margarine or butter for brushing grill rack
1	medium-sized tomato, sliced, for garnish
	Fresh basil leaves for garnish (optional)

For sauce, put basil, nuts, garlic, and salt in a food processor fitted with steel blade or a blender. Process until pureed. With the machine running, pour oil through the feed tube in a slow, steady stream. Process until sauce is smooth. Spoon sauce into a bowl. Cover and refrigerate.

Cover bread with slices of Brie cheese. Spread top of cheese with a thin layer of sauce.

Prepare the grill, and when the coals are hot, place bread on grill rack, brushed with margarine, about 4 to 6 inches from heat source. Cover and grill for 1 to 2 minutes. Bread will be toasted on the bottom, and cheese will be soft and runny. Place two pieces of toast on each plate and garnish with tomato slices and basil leaves. Serve hot.

Figs Stuffed with Edam Cheese

8 servings

1	cup ½-inch cubes of Edam cheese
½	cup ground almonds
24	soft dried figs or fresh figs, cut in half but still attached at one end
	Melted margarine or butter for brushing grill rack
	Seedless green grapes for garnish
	Candied almonds for garnish

In a small bowl, mix cheese with ground almonds. With a small spoon or your hands, stuff figs with cheese, using about two pieces of cheese per fig, and gently press each fig back together.

Prepare the grill, and when the coals are hot, place figs on grill rack, brushed with margarine, about 4 to 6 inches from heat source. Grill figs for 3 minutes, rotating once. When done, figs will be hot and cheese soft.

Place stuffed figs on a serving dish and garnish with grapes and almonds.

Prosciutto and Melon
with Swiss Cheese

Although prosciutto with melon is usually served cold, the combination is a real treat grilled and served hot or warm.

6 servings

12	1- by 6-inch thin slices Swiss cheese
6	slices prosciutto, cut in half
1	small cantaloupe or honeydew melon, peeled and cut into 12 ½-inch slices
3	tablespoons canola oil
½	teaspoon dried oregano
	Canola oil for brushing grill rack
3	tablespoons drained capers for garnish
2	lemons, sliced, for garnish

Place a piece of cheese on each piece of prosciutto. Wrap the layered prosciutto and cheese around each piece of melon. Mix 3 tablespoons oil with oregano and lightly brush the prosciutto. Refrigerate wrapped melon until the coals are ready.

Prepare the grill, and when the coals are hot, place wrapped melon on grill rack, brushed with oil, about 4 to 6 inches from heat source. Grill prosciutto for about 3 to 4 minutes, turning once. Prosciutto and melon will be warm and beginning to brown.

To serve, place two pieces of grilled prosciutto and melon on each dish, sprinkle with capers, and add a slice of lemon. Serve immediately.

Flameless Greek Cheese

The cheese slices for this recipe can be prepared a day ahead and chilled overnight.

8 servings

1	cup milk
1	egg white, slightly beaten
1½	cups fresh fine bread crumbs
½	pound saganaki (Greek melting cheese), cut into 8 equal ½-inch slices

Garlic Pita Chips

3	tablespoons margarine or butter
¼	teaspoon garlic powder
3	pita breads, each split into 2 rounds

	Olive oil for brushing grill rack
2	tablespoons Metaxa brandy
2	lemons, sliced thin, for garnish

Mix milk and egg white in a shallow bowl. Place bread crumbs on a plate. Roll cheese slices in milk mixture and then in bread crumbs. Set cheese on a dish and refrigerate for at least 45 minutes.

For garlic pita chips, mix margarine and garlic powder. Brush pita bread with mixture.

Prepare the grill, and when the coals are hot, toast pita on grill. Cut into quarters.

Place cheese on grill rack, brushed with oil, about 4 to 6 inches from the heat source. Warm cheese for about 2 minutes, turning after 1 minute. Cheese will be soft, runny, and lightly browned on the outside.

To serve, divide cheese among individual plates, sprinkle lightly with Metaxa brandy, and garnish with lemon slices. Serve hot with garlic pita chips or other crusty bread.

Cheese Terrine with Grilled Red Pepper/Tomato Sauce

My close friend, Eunice Tobin, is an outstanding cook, humorist, and writer. She generously contributed this recipe.

6 to 8 servings

Terrine

3	tablespoons butter or margarine
6	tablespoons fresh bread crumbs
½	pound cream cheese at room temperature, cut into chunks
½	pound cottage cheese
¼	cup milk or half-and-half
2	teaspoons cornstarch
2	eggs
1	cup chopped chives
½	cup chopped pitted black olives
½	pound prosciutto, chopped
	Boiling water

Grilled Red Pepper/Tomato Sauce

6	plum tomatoes
1	large red bell pepper, seeded and cut into quarters
1	medium-sized onion, cut into quarters
	Olive oil for brushing grill rack

Brush a 4-inch by 8-inch loaf pan with butter or margarine. Sprinkle pan with bread crumbs, pressing them onto the bottom and sides of the pan. Set aside.

Using an electric mixer, blend cream cheese with cottage cheese, milk, cornstarch, and eggs until smooth. Mix in chives, olives, and prosciutto. Spoon cheese mixture into prepared pan. Cover pan with aluminum foil.

Preheat oven to 350 degrees. Set a pan, larger than the loaf pan, in the oven and set the pan in the center. Pour boiling water into the pan around the terrine. Bake for 1 hour. Cool terrine in oven with door open. Refrigerate overnight. The terrine can be prepared the day before serving.

Discard foil. Run a small sharp knife around the perimeter of the terrine. Invert onto a serving plate. Place a hot dish cloth on terrine to loosen it. Slice terrine while cold.

When ready to serve, prepare the grill. Using two double-pronged skewers, thread tomatoes onto one skewer and pepper and onion pieces onto second skewer. When the coals are hot, place skewered vegetables on a grill rack, brushed with oil, about 4 to 6 inches from heat source. Grill skewered vegetables for 5 minutes, turning once.

Empty skewered vegetables into a food processor fitted with steel blade. Process until pureed.

To serve, spoon sauce onto individual plates and top sauce with a thin slice of cheese terrine. Serve immediately.

Nachos Grande

For a special treat, try blue corn chips in this recipe. Be sure to wear rubber gloves when handling jalapeños and be careful not to touch your eyes. You can buy the salsa or make your own (see Index).

8 servings

1	16-ounce bag tortilla chips
3	cups shredded Monterey Jack cheese
¼	cup (or to taste) chopped fresh jalapeño peppers
1	cup plain nonfat yogurt or sour cream
1	cup salsa
2	avocados, peeled, pits discarded, chopped
2	tablespoons freshly squeezed lemon juice

Cut a double thickness of aluminum foil large enough to hold the chips. Set chips in center of foil. Sprinkle with cheese and top with jalapeño peppers. Close foil securely and set aside.

Prepare the grill for the indirect method. When the coals are hot, pour hot water into the pan between the coals. Replace grill about 4 to 6 inches from heat source and set foil bag in center of grill. Cover grill and cook nachos for 3 to 5 minutes or until cheese has melted.

To serve, transfer nachos to a large serving dish. Serve with yogurt, salsa, and avocado sprinkled with lemon juice. Serve hot.

MEAT

Ground Lamb with Sunflower Seeds on a Mint Skewer

In the fall or late summer you can use woody herb stems for skewers to impart a subtle flavor to food. Remove the leaves and make a point at one end of the stem. In this recipe mint stems are used as skewers.

8 servings

1½	pounds lean ground lamb
2	tablespoons olive oil or canola oil
1	small onion, chopped
3	tablespoons minced fresh parsley
¼	teaspoon salt
½	teaspoon freshly ground pepper
2	tablespoons freshly squeezed lemon juice
¼	cup cooked rice
¼	teaspoon ground cinnamon
¼	teaspoon ground allspice
3	teaspoons chopped fresh or dried mint
¾	cup sunflower kernels, plus extra for garnish
	Canola oil for brushing grill rack

In a mixing bowl, combine ground lamb with all the ingredients except canola oil for rack. Divide mixture into eight equal portions. Form meat around bamboo skewers, soaked in cold water for 15 minutes and drained, or use mint stick skewers. If you are using mint skewers, wrap ends with foil so they do not burn. Refrigerate prepared skewers until coals are hot.

Prepare the grill, and when the coals are hot, place the ground lamb on grill rack, brushed with oil, about 4 to 6 inches from heat source. Grill lamb for about 6 minutes or until just cooked through.

Transfer meat to individual plates and sprinkle with extra sunflower seeds. Serve hot.

Baby Back Ribs with Brown Sugar Barbecue Sauce

Allow about six ribs per person for an appetizer. Serve with Black Pepper Corn Bread Sticks (recipe follows).

8 servings

Brown Sugar Barbecue Sauce

3	strips bacon, cut into 1-inch pieces
1	cup minced scallions
3	cloves garlic, minced
¾	cup catsup
1	16-ounce can tomatoes, with juice, chopped
¼	cup red wine vinegar
⅓	cup firmly packed dark brown sugar
2	teaspoons chili powder
⅛	teaspoon ground cloves
1	teaspoon grated orange zest
	Juice from 1 orange
½	teaspoon salt
½	teaspoon hot red pepper flakes
½	teaspoon freshly ground pepper
4	pounds (about 3 slabs) baby back ribs, simmered in water to cover for 10 minutes and drained

For sauce, cook bacon in a medium saucepan until crisp. Leave bacon in pan and discard all but 3 tablespoons bacon fat. Add scallions and garlic and sauté over low heat for 3 minutes, stirring occasionally. Stir in remaining sauce ingredients. Simmer sauce for 5 to 8 minutes, stirring occasionally. Taste and adjust seasonings. Cool, puree in a blender, and pour into a bowl. Cover and refrigerate until needed.

Prepare the grill, and when the coals are hot, brush ribs generously with the sauce. Set ribs on grill rack abut 4 to 6 inches from the heat source. Grill for about 20 to 30 minutes or until done, turning occasionally. During last 10 minutes of cooking, brush ribs with sauce. When ribs are done, remove them to a cutting board. Cut rack into individual ribs.

Place six ribs on each plate and serve hot with corn bread and extra barbecue sauce.

Black Pepper Corn Bread Sticks

This corn bread is made in a heavy iron corn stick pan and is cooked on the grill using preheated tiles.

8 servings

	Margarine or butter for greasing pan
1½	cups yellow cornmeal
½	cup all-purpose flour
1½	teaspoons baking powder
¾	teaspoon baking soda
½	teaspoon salt
½	teaspoon freshly ground pepper
2	teaspoons sugar
2	eggs, slightly beaten
1½	cups milk
2	tablespoons margarine or butter, melted and cooled
1	small red bell pepper, seeded and chopped

Prepare the grill, and while the coals are heating, grease an eight-hole corn stick pan. In a large mixing bowl, mix cornmeal, flour, baking powder, baking soda, salt, pepper, and sugar just until combined. Do not overbeat batter. Mix in egg, milk, and melted margarine.

Pour mixture carefully into greased pan. Set tiles on the hot grill and preheat. Place pan on tiles. Cover grill and cook for 20 minutes or until a cake tester inserted in one of the corn bread sticks comes out dry. Remove from grill, cool for 5 minutes, and remove from pan. Serve hot or reheat, wrapped in a double thickness of aluminum foil, on outer edges of grill for 3 minutes or until warm.

Old-Fashioned Potato Salad

8 to 10 servings

6	large potatoes, peeled, boiled in salted water, cooled, and diced
6	strips bacon, cut into 1-inch pieces
1	medium-sized red onion, minced
3	ribs celery, diced
1½	tablespoons all-purpose flour
¼	teaspoon sugar
¼	teaspoon minced fresh parsley
½	teaspoon salt
½	teaspoon celery seeds
¼	teaspoon freshly ground white pepper
½	cup water
⅓	cup cider vinegar

Put potatoes in a deep bowl and set aside. Fry bacon over medium heat, stirring occasionally, until crisp. Drain bacon on paper towels and leave 2 tablespoons of the bacon drippings in the pan. Sauté onion and celery in bacon drippings (or in canola oil) for about 5 minutes or until tender, stirring occasionally.

Whisk in flour, sugar, parsley, salt, celery seeds, and pepper. Cook for 1 minute over medium heat. Stir in water and vinegar. Boil dressing for 1 minute longer. Add crumbled bacon pieces. Toss potatoes with dressing.

Serve potato salad hot.

Lamb Sausage with Hot Sauce

Serve lamb sausage with Old-Fashioned Potato Salad (recipe follows).

8 servings

Horseradish Sauce

6	medium-sized tomatoes, peeled, seeded, and pureed
1	medium-sized onion, minced
1	medium-sized red bell pepper, seeded and chopped
2½	teaspoons pickling spices, wrapped in a cheesecloth bag
3	tablespoons dark brown sugar
¼	teaspoon salt
2	teaspoons prepared white horseradish

Lamb Sausage

1¾	pounds lean lamb
½	cup fresh fine bread crumbs
1	egg white, slightly beaten
1	medium-sized onion, minced
¼	cup chopped fresh dill
½	teaspoon celery seeds
½	cup chopped green or red bell pepper
½	teaspoon salt
¼	teaspoon freshly ground pepper
	Canola oil for brushing grill rack

For sauce, mix tomatoes and onion in a medium saucepan. Mix in bell pepper, spice bag, brown sugar, salt, and horseradish. Bring to a boil over medium heat. Reduce to simmer and cook for 10 minutes, partially covered. Taste and adjust seasonings. Cool. Place sauce in a covered container and refrigerate.

For sausage, crumble lamb into a bowl. Mix in remaining sausage ingredients and shape mixture into 3-inch sausages. Set on a dish and refrigerate until ready to grill. Remove sauce from refrigerator so it can come to room temperature or reheat sauce while lamb sausage cools.

Prepare the grill, and when the coals are hot, set lamb sausage on grill rack, brushed with oil, about 4 to 6 inches from heat source. Grill lamb sausages for 2 to 3 minutes on each side or until done to taste. Lamb sausage will brown slightly and should be cooked medium or to taste.

Transfer lamb sausages to a serving dish or individual plates. Serve with horse-radish sauce, mixed well, and grilled pita bread.

Oriental Pork Slices

Hoisin sauce is a Chinese sauce that is favored by my family, especially my daughter, Dorothy. Spicy and sweet, it is a thick sauce made from soybeans, garlic, water, chili, flour, and spices. Refrigerate it after it is opened.

8 to 10 servings
Hoisin Marinade

½	cup dry white wine
2	cloves garlic, minced
2	tablespoons sugar
⅓	cup light soy sauce
⅓	cup hoisin sauce

1¾ to 2 pounds pork tenderloin
Honey Brushing Sauce

¼	cup light soy sauce
¼	cup honey
½	teaspoon Oriental (dark) sesame oil

For marinade, combine wine, garlic, sugar, soy sauce, and hoisin sauce. Put pork in a large self-sealing bag and add marinade. Seal bag securely and turn several times so that all areas of pork are touched by marinade. Marinate pork in refrigerator for 3 to 4 hours, turning occasionally.

For brushing sauce, mix soy sauce, honey, and sesame oil.

Prepare the grill, and when the coals are hot, remove pork from marinade. Place pork on grill rack about 4 to 6 inches from heat source. Grill pork for 8 to 9 minutes or until done, turning and brushing pork with honey brushing sauce every 2 to 3 minutes. Pork will be cooked through and golden brown on the outside.

Transfer pork to a platter and let stand for 5 minutes. Cut pork into thin slices. This dish is good hot or cold. Serve with grilled scallions.

Barbecued Whole Salami

You can substitute low-calorie jam for the marmalade in this recipe and use any kind of salami you like.

8 to 10 servings

¾ cup orange marmalade or apricot preserves
2 tablespoons water
2 tablespoons stone-ground mustard
1 2-pound salami, peeled
½ cup fresh Italian parsley sprigs
1 cup pitted black olives
2 cups cherry tomatoes

Mix marmalade with water and simmer until mixture is smooth, about 2 to 3 minutes, stirring often. Cool mixture. Blend in mustard.

Prepare the grill, and when the coals are hot, brush salami with marmalade mixture. Set salami on grill rack about 4 to 6 inches from heat source. Cover and grill salami for 15 minutes, turning it every 2 to 3 minutes. Salami will be hot and browned on the outside when done.

Transfer salami to a cutting board. Slice thin and arrange on a serving plate. Sprinkle with Italian parsley, black olives, and tomatoes. Serve hot or cold.

Cantonese Stuffed Peppers

8 servings

½   pound lean ground beef
½   teaspoon ground ginger
2   cloves garlic, minced
¼   teaspoon salt
¼   teaspoon freshly ground pepper
2   scallions, minced
3   tablespoons minced water chestnuts
2   tablespoons dry white wine
2   teaspoons light soy sauce
4   large red bell peppers, seeded and quartered along their natural lines

Put ground beef into a deep bowl. Mix in ginger, garlic, salt, pepper, scallions, water chestnuts, wine, and soy sauce. Stuff mixture into pepper quarters.

Prepare the grill, and when the coals are hot, set stuffed peppers, meat side down, on grill rack, about 4 to 6 inches from heat source. Cook stuffed peppers for 3 minutes. Using a long-handled spatula, turn each pepper over and continue grilling for 1 minute or until meat is cooked through. Peppers will be charred.

Transfer peppers to a serving dish and serve hot. Try serving with whole scallions, lightly oiled and grilled for 1 to 2 minutes on each side.

SMOKED DELIGHTS

Smoked Whitefish

Always prepare your smoker according to the manufacturer's directions. I fill my fuel pan about two-thirds full, and I find hardwood charcoal gives the best results.

8 servings

2   lemons, sliced
8   small whitefish, about 6 to 8 ounces each, *or* 1 whole whitefish,
       about 2½ pounds, cleaned and scaled
3   pieces cherry or other fruit wood, soaked in cold water for
       1 hour and drained

Put lemon slices in fish cavity.

Prepare smoker according to manufacturer's directions. When coals are hot, add drained wood. Using pot holders, set water pan, about two-thirds full of hot water, in place.

Place fish on grill, cover, and smoke for 45 minutes to 1 hour for small fish or 2 hours for a large fish. When done, fish will flake easily when prodded with tines of a fork. Check smoker after 1 hour to see if more coals or water is needed.

For small fish, place one on each plate. For a large fish, you may want to set it on a tray and serve it whole on a bed of lettuce or skin it and divide into chunks. This fish is good served with sliced tomatoes, scallions, and warm rolls.

Smoked Salmon with Cheese and Bagels

8 servings

1½ to 2	pounds salmon fillet, boned, skin on
	Canola oil for brushing salmon
3	cups hickory chips, soaked in cold water for 1 hour and drained
1	lemon, sliced thin
½	pound cream cheese or creamed cottage cheese
3	large tomatoes, sliced
1	medium-sized red onion, sliced thin
1	cup pitted black olives
¼	head lettuce, cleaned and separated into leaves
16	small bagels, sliced in half

Brush salmon with oil and set aside.

Prepare smoker according to manufacturer's directions. When coals are hot, sprinkle with drained wood. Using pot holders, set water pan, about two-thirds full of hot water, in place.

Place lemon slices on grill. Set salmon over lemon slices. Cover and smoke salmon for about 45 minutes to 1 hour. Salmon will lose its translucent look and flake easily when prodded with tines of a fork.

When salmon is smoked, transfer it to a serving tray and serve warm or cold. Arrange cream cheese, tomato, onion, olives, lettuce, and bagels on a tray and serve. Good for brunch or as an appetizer.

Smoked Fish Pâté

8 servings

1	pound center-cut trout, boneless, skin on
	Canola oil for brushing trout
3	pieces applewood or hickory, 6 to 8 inches long, soaked in cold water for 1 hour and drained
1	small pear, peeled, cored, and chopped
¼	cup minced onion
¼	teaspoon dried sage
¼	teaspoon hot red pepper flakes
1	clove garlic, minced
¼	teaspoon salt

Brush trout with oil and set aside.

Prepare smoker according to manufacturer's directions. When coals are hot, add drained wood. Using pot holders, set water pan, about two-thirds full of hot water, in place.

Place trout on grill rack. Cover and cook trout for 45 minutes or until done to taste. Fish will be a golden color and will flake easily when prodded with tines of a fork.

Remove skin and bones from trout. Flake fish and place in a bowl. Mix in pear, onion, sage, red pepper, garlic, and salt. Mix pâté until all ingredients are combined. Spoon into a serving bowl. The pâté can be served immediately or covered and refrigerated for later use. Serve with crudités such as carrot sticks, pepper slices, scallions, and other vegetables of your choice and crackers.

Smoked Mussels
with Herb Mayonnaise

*Homemade mayonnaise tastes better than store-bought, but it does not keep long.
Use it as soon as possible and keep refrigerated until serving time.*

8 servings

Herb Mayonnaise

1	egg
1	tablespoon freshly squeezed lemon juice
2	teaspoons cider vinegar
1	teaspoon minced fresh parsley
½	teaspoon minced fresh basil
¼	teaspoon salt
¼	teaspoon freshly ground white pepper
1	cup olive oil

32	green-lip mussels, scrubbed and debearded
3	cups fruit wood branches broken into 5-inch pieces, soaked in cold water for 1 hour and drained

For mayonnaise, put egg, lemon juice, vinegar, parsley, basil, salt, and pepper in a food processor fitted with steel blade or a blender. Process until combined. With machine running, pour in oil in a slow, steady stream. Continue processing until mixture is thick and well mixed. Spoon into a serving dish and use immediately or refrigerate and use as soon as possible.

Prepare smoker according to manufacturer's directions. When coals are hot, add drained wood. Using pot holders, set water pan, about two-thirds full of hot water, in place.

Set mussels on grill and cover. Smoke mussels for about 6 to 10 minutes. Discard any unopened mussels.

Put mussels on individual plates and serve with a dollop of mayonnaise. Mussels are good hot or warm.

Hickory-Smoked Baby Back Ribs

Ribs are good served with garlic bread. Slice bread and brush with melted marga-rine or butter mixed with crushed garlic to taste. Warm bread over hot grill.

6 to 8 servings

3 to 4	pounds baby back ribs, in slabs

Beer Barbecue Sauce

2	tablespoons peanut oil or canola oil
3	cloves garlic, minced
4	scallions, minced
¾	cup beer
¼	cup red wine vinegar
⅓	cup catsup
1	cup tomato juice
1	teaspoon Worcestershire sauce
½	teaspoon prepared mustard
¼	cup firmly packed light brown sugar
1	teaspoon chili powder
1	teaspoon ground cumin
3	cups hickory chips, soaked in cold water for 1 hour and drained
	Canola oil for brushing grill rack

Fill a large kettle with enough water to cover ribs. Add ribs, bring to a boil, lower heat, and simmer for 10 minutes. Remove ribs from water.

While ribs are simmering, prepare sauce. Heat oil in a saucepan. Add garlic and scallions and sauté over medium heat for 4 minutes, stirring occasionally. Stir in remaining sauce ingredients. Reduce heat to simmer and continue cooking for 5 minutes, stirring once or twice. Cool sauce.

Brush ribs with some of the sauce and place them in a glass dish. Let ribs stand for 1 hour.

Prepare smoker according to manufacturer's directions. When coals are hot, sprinkle with drained wood. Using pot holders, set water pan, about two-thirds full of hot water, in place.

Brush ribs with sauce again and set on a rack brushed with oil. Cover smoker. Cook ribs for about 1 hour. Ribs will be tender.

Transfer slabs to a cutting board and cut into single ribs. Divide ribs among individual plates and brush generously with barbecue sauce. Serve hot.

Smoked Freshwater Caviar and Gruyère Cheese on Noodles

8 servings

½	pound whitefish freshwater caviar
½	pound Gruyère cheese
3	cups applewood, soaked in cold water for 1 hour and drained
1	pound angel hair pasta, cooked al dente and drained
¼	cup margarine or butter
2	cups plain nonfat yogurt
½	teaspoon dried thyme
½	teaspoon salt
¼	teaspoon freshly ground white pepper

Put caviar in an ovenproof ceramic dish and cover with aluminum foil. Poke holes in foil with a fork. Wrap cheese in aluminum foil.

Prepare smoker according to manufacturer's directions. When the coals are hot, sprinkle with drained wood. Using pot holders, set water pan, about two-thirds full of hot water, in place.

Place caviar and cheese on top rack. Cover smoker and smoke food for 20 minutes. Remove caviar and cheese from smoker. Cheese will be soft and smoky in flavor. Immediately place in refrigerator to firm.

Refresh pasta by running hot water over it. Drain pasta, place it in a bowl and toss with butter. Spoon yogurt into a small bowl. Mix in thyme, salt, and pepper. Toss yogurt dressing with pasta.

Divide pasta among eight small plates. Slice cheese into eight portions. Set one piece of cheese on each plate. Sprinkle caviar on top of pasta. Serve at once.

SANDWICHES

New England Baked Beans

My New England heritage shows through in the following recipe. New England Baked Beans can be prepared up to 2 days ahead of time, making entertaining a snap. They taste great alongside sandwiches. For this recipe it is not necessary to soak the beans overnight.

8 to 10 servings

1	pound dry pinto beans, washed and picked over, shriveled beans removed
1	medium-sized onion, chopped
¼	pound salt pork or bacon, cut into 1-inch cubes
¾	cup molasses
2	tablespoons dark brown sugar
¼	cup catsup
1	teaspoon prepared mustard
¼	teaspoon ground ginger
2	teaspoons salt

Place beans and onion in a large pan and cover with 2 to 3 inches of water. Bring water to a boil, reduce heat, and simmer, covered, until beans are fork-tender. It may be necessary to add more hot water to keep beans covered. Beans will be tender in about 2 hours and 45 minutes to 3 hours. Cool. Drain beans and reserve liquid.

Preheat oven to 300 degrees. Transfer beans to a bean pot or other ovenproof casserole. Stir in remaining ingredients. Add just enough reserved cooking liquid to cover the beans. Cover and bake for 2 hours and 45 minutes to 3 hours, stirring every 30 minutes and removing cover after 2 hours. Taste and adjust seasonings. Serve hot.

Southern Pork Barbecue Sandwiches

This sandwich is great served with New England Baked Beans (recipe follows).

8 servings

Chili Marinade

½ cup peanut oil or canola oil
¾ cup red wine vinegar
¼ cup firmly packed light brown sugar
½ teaspoon ground cumin
¾ teaspoon chili powder
1 clove garlic, minced
¼ teaspoon freshly ground pepper

2 pounds boneless pork loin, trimmed and excess fat discarded

Brushing Sauce

3 tablespoons peanut oil or canola oil
1 large onion, minced
1 cup catsup
2 medium-sized tomatoes, peeled, seeded, and chopped
¼ cup whiskey
1 teaspoon chili powder
¼ teaspoon Tabasco sauce
5 tablespoons firmly packed light brown sugar
2 tablespoons freshly squeezed lime juice
¼ teaspoon salt
½ cup tomato juice

3 cups hickory chips, soaked in cold water for 1 hour and drained
8 hamburger buns or other sandwich rolls

Combine marinade ingredients and pour into a glass dish large enough to hold pork loin. Place pork in marinade and turn several times so that all surfaces touch marinade. Cover lightly and refrigerate. Marinate for 5 to 6 hours, turning occasionally.

While pork is marinating, prepare sauce. Heat oil in a saucepan, add onion, and sauté over medium heat for 4 minutes, stirring occasionally. Stir in remaining sauce ingredients and blend well. Bring sauce to a boil, reduce heat, and simmer for 6 to 8 minutes, stirring occasionally. Taste and adjust seasonings. Remove from heat, cool, puree in a blender or processor, and pour into a bowl. Cover lightly and refrigerate until needed.

Prepare smoker according to manufacturer's directions. When coals are hot, add drained wood. Drain pork and set on lowest rack. Brush with sauce, cover, and smoke pork for about 2 hours, brushing with sauce every 30 minutes and checking it after 1½ hours. Pork is done when juices run clear when meat is cut with sharp point of knife. Check coals and water after an hour to see if they have to be replenished.

Transfer pork to cutting board and let it stand for 5 minutes. Using a sharp knife, carefully shred pork. Brush generously with remaining sauce. Spoon pork onto warm buns, and serve with baked beans and coleslaw. Some people like to add the coleslaw to the sandwich. Serve hot.

Bites of Lamb in Warm Pita Bread

8 or more servings

Mediterranean Marinade

¾	cup olive oil
4	cloves garlic, crushed
½	cup red wine
¼	teaspoon freshly ground pepper
2	teaspoons dried oregano
1	teaspoon dried basil

2½ to 3	pounds butterflied leg of lamb, cut into 1-inch pieces
8	cherry tomatoes
2	medium-sized red bell peppers, seeded and sliced
	Olive oil for brushing peppers
2	cups plain nonfat yogurt
1	tablespoon minced onion
1	tablespoon chopped fresh mint
4	or more whole-wheat pita breads, cut in half crosswise to make pockets

Soak eight bamboo skewers or oregano stem skewers in cold water for 15 minutes; drain.

Mix marinade ingredients in a bowl. Pour marinade evenly into two large self-sealing plastic bags. Add meat and seal bags securely. Turn bags several times so that meat is covered or touched by marinade. Set bag in a shallow dish in refrigerator for 4 to 6 hours, turning meat two or three times.

Prepare the grill, and when the coals are hot, drain meat, reserving marinade. Thread meat on skewers, ending each skewer with a cherry tomato. Set kabobs on a grill rack about 4 to 6 inches from heat source. Brush pepper strips with oil and add to grill rack. Grill kabobs for about 9 minutes, turning and brushing with reserved marinade every 3 minutes or until lamb is pink in the center or done to taste. Turn peppers as needed, grilling until lightly charred.

Mix yogurt with onion and mint.

Transfer lamb to a plate. Warm pita bread on grill rack. Open bread and fill with lamb, tomatoes, and grilled peppers. Serve hot. Pass yogurt dressing at the table as a condiment.

Pork Kabobs on Italian Bread

6 servings

Tomato Juice Marinade

¾ cup olive oil
3 cloves garlic, crushed
½ cup cider vinegar
¼ cup chopped fresh mint
½ teaspoon hot red pepper flakes
3 tablespoons minced fresh parsley
1 teaspoon dried oregano

2 pounds pork tenderloin, cut into ¾-inch cubes
¾ cup tomato juice
1 10- to 12-inch loaf Italian bread, split lengthwise and sliced into 6 sections
1 cup mild pickled Italian sweet peppers
Lettuce leaves
Sliced tomatoes
Sliced pitted black olives

Soak six bamboo skewers in cold water for 15 minutes; drain.

Mix marinade ingredients in a bowl. Pour marinade evenly into two large self-sealing plastic bags. Divide pork pieces between bags and seal securely. Turn bags several times so that all surfaces of pork are touched by marinade. Set bags in a shallow glass dish and marinate in refrigerator for 24 hours. Four or 5 hours before grilling time, add tomato juice to marinade.

Prepare the grill, and when the coals are hot, drain pork pieces and reserve marinade as a brushing sauce. Thread pork pieces evenly onto skewers. Set kabobs on grill rack about 4 to 6 inches from heat source. Grill kabobs for about 9 minutes or until pork is done to taste, turning and brushing with reserved marinade every 3 minutes. All traces of pink should have disappeared, yet the pork should not be overcooked.

Transfer pork to a tray and bring to the table hot. Warm the bread, cut side down, on the grill for 1 to 2 minutes or until toasted. Have guests make their own sandwiches by removing pork from skewers and placing it on bread. Serve with peppers, lettuce, tomatoes, and black olives.

Spaghetti Bread Cheese Sandwiches

These sandwiches can be made with regular or whole-wheat bread. For a special treat, try the spaghetti bread. When my daughter Dorothy was a little girl, we used to make this bread often.

6 servings

Bread

1	¼-ounce package active dry yeast
½	cup warm water
2	teaspoons sugar
3	cups all-purpose flour
½	teaspoon salt
1	tablespoon margarine or butter, melted
2	eggs, slightly beaten
½	cup leftover spaghetti with a little sauce still clinging to the pasta
1	egg white, slightly beaten
	Freshly grated Parmesan cheese to sprinkle over bread

Sandwiches

1	pound cheddar cheese, sliced thin
2	medium-sized red onions, sliced thin
	Melted margarine or butter for brushing grill rack and sandwiches
¾	cup dried oregano, soaked in cold water for 10 minutes and drained, as an aromatic

For bread, sprinkle yeast over warm water and sugar. Let stand in a warm area for 5 minutes or until mixture begins to bubble.

Place flour in a mixing bowl. Stir in salt, margarine, and eggs. Blend in yeast mixture. Mix until dough is well blended. Shape dough into a ball and place in a bowl. Cover lightly and let rise in a draft-free area until double in size, about 45 minutes to 1 hour. Punch dough down on lightly floured board and stir in spaghetti so that it is evenly distributed.

Shape bread into a loaf. Set dough in a well-greased loaf pan and set at room temperature in a draft-free area for about 45 minutes or until bread has doubled in size.

Preheat oven to 375 degrees. Bake bread for 20 minutes. Brush bread with egg white and sprinkle with Parmesan cheese. Continue baking the bread until done, about 20 to 25 minutes. The bread will make a hollow sound when tapped with your fingers. Remove bread from pan and cool on a wire rack.

Cut 12 slices of bread. Make six sandwiches with the bread and cheese. Brush sandwiches and onion slices lightly with melted margarine.

Sprinkle drained oregano over hot coals and quickly place grill rack, brushed with margarine, about 4 to 6 inches from heat source. Grill sandwiches and onion rings on rack for about 3 to 4 minutes, turning once. Cheese will be soft and runny, and bread and onion rings will be lightly browned.

Serve sandwiches hot, sliced in half, with the grilled onions.

Hickory-Smoked Chuck Roast Sandwiches

Serve these hickory-smoked sandwiches with refreshing Cucumber Salad with Walnuts (recipe follows).

8 to 10 servings

Garlic Marinade

½	cup canola oil
⅓	cup light soy sauce
1	medium-sized onion, sliced
3	cloves garlic, minced
1	teaspoon grated fresh gingeroot
1	teaspoon stone-ground mustard
⅓	cup red wine
⅓	cup catsup

2½	pounds boneless lean chuck roast
3	cups hickory chips, soaked in cold water for 1 hour and drained
2	cups Smoky Barbecue Sauce (see Index) *or* prepared sauce
8 to 10	sesame seed hamburger buns or hard rolls
	Pickles
	Coleslaw
	Sliced tomatoes

Mix marinade ingredients in a bowl. Set meat in a glass casserole or other large glass dish. Pour marinade over meat. Cover lightly and refrigerate for 6 hours, turning meat once or twice.

Prepare smoker according to manufacturer's directions. When coals are hot, add drained wood. Remove meat from marinade and drain. Set meat on grill and cover smoker. Cook for about 2 hours.

Transfer meat to platter and cut into it to test for doneness (or use a meat thermometer).

Transfer meat to a carving board and let stand for 5 to 10 minutes. Slice into paper-thin slices across the grain and place in a bowl. Stir in the barbecue sauce.

Mound meat slices on warm buns. Serve hot with pickles, coleslaw, and sliced tomatoes.

Shrimp Po-Boys

A wonderful trip to New Orleans is responsible for my interpretation of the Po-Boys and the Muffulettas (see Index) on the grill.

6 servings

6	individual French bread rolls, cut in half lengthwise
	Olive oil or canola oil for brushing grill rack, rolls, and shrimp
2	cups yellow cornmeal
¼	teaspoon salt
¼	teaspoon dried thyme
¼	teaspoon hot red pepper flakes
1¾	pounds large shrimp, peeled and deveined
6	lettuce leaves
3	medium-sized tomatoes, sliced
1	medium-sized red onion, chopped, for garnish

Lightly brush cut side of French rolls with oil and set aside.

Spread cornmeal on a flat plate. Mix in salt, thyme, and red pepper. Lightly dust shrimp with cornmeal mixture.

Prepare the grill, and when the coals are hot, place shrimp on grill rack, brushed with oil, about 4 to 6 inches from heat source. Grill shrimp, for about 4 to 5 minutes, turning once or twice. Shrimp are done when they turn a whitish color and are opaque. Do not overcook shrimp, or they will become tough and rubbery. While shrimp are grilling, heat rolls on grill, cut side down, for 1 to 2 minutes. Rolls should be warm and slightly toasted.

To serve, put a lettuce leaf on a heated roll. Arrange shrimp and tomato slices over lettuce. Sprinkle lightly with chopped onion. Serve sandwiches hot.

Cucumber Salad with Walnuts

Although cucumber spears are also delicious on the grill, try this Mediterranean salad as a sandwich accompaniment. It is refreshing and can be prepared the day before serving.

8 servings

2 large cucumbers, peeled and sliced thin
1 large red onion, sliced thin
2 cups plain nonfat yogurt
½ teaspoon salt
2 cloves garlic, minced
2 tablespoons olive oil
¼ cup chopped fresh mint *or* ¾ teaspoon dried
⅓ cup chopped walnuts for garnish

Place cucumbers in a ceramic salad bowl. Toss with onion slices. Stir in yogurt, salt, garlic, oil, and mint. Cover lightly and refrigerate until serving time.
Stir salad before serving and sprinkle with chopped walnuts.

Barbecued Beef Sandwiches

Marinade

½   cup olive oil or canola oil
1½   cups beer
¼   cup firmly packed light brown sugar
¾   teaspoon chili powder
¼   cup minced fresh parsley
¼   teaspoon ground allspice

1   beef sirloin steak, about 2½ pounds, excess fat trimmed off

Smoky Barbecue Sauce

2   tablespoons olive oil
3   cloves garlic, minced
1   16-ounce can stewed tomatoes, including juice
1   cup catsup
¼   cup cider vinegar
½   cup light brown sugar
1   tablespoon chili powder
1   teaspoon ground cumin
$1/8$ teaspoon ground cinnamon
½   teaspoon (or to taste) liquid smoke

3   cups mesquite or other wood chips, soaked in cold water for
        1 hour and drained
    Canola oil for brushing grill rack
6   French bread rolls, hard rolls, or rye rolls

Combine marinade ingredients in a bowl. Pour marinade into a shallow glass dish. Set trimmed steak in marinade and cover lightly with plastic wrap. Marinate for 4 to 5 hours in refrigerator, turning once or twice.

While meat is marinating, prepare the sauce. Heat oil in a saucepan. Add garlic and sauté over low heat for 1 minute. Stir in remaining sauce ingredients and simmer for 5 minutes, stirring occasionally. Set sauce aside.

Prepare the grill, and when the coals are hot, drain steak, discarding marinade. Sprinkle drained wood chips over hot coals and quickly place steak on grill rack, brushed with oil, 4 to 6 inches from heat source. Grill steak for 1½ to 2 minutes on each side, then continue grilling for 5 minutes on each side or until meat is just pink or done to taste. To test for doneness, transfer meat to a platter and cut into its thickest section (or use meat thermometer).

Set meat on a carving tray and let stand for 5 to 10 minutes. Reheat sauce to warm if necessary. Cut meat into paper-thin slices across the grain. Place shredded meat in a deep bowl. Stir in warm barbecue sauce. Slice rolls in half and warm on grill if desired. Set rolls on dinner plates and spoon warm beef with sauce over the rolls. Serve immediately.

Muffulettas

The Muffuletta is a New Orleans creation. First you prepare marinated vegetable salad. Then arrange the meat and cheese with the vegetables on a French bread roll. In this recipe you marinate your own vegetables and heat the sandwich on the grill for that special smoky flavor.

6 servings

Marinated Olive Salad

¾	cup olive oil
4	cloves garlic, minced
1¾	cups chopped cauliflower
1¾	cups chopped broccoli
1	medium-sized green bell pepper, seeded and chopped
1	medium-sized onion, chopped
2	cups pimiento-stuffed green olives, chopped and ¾ cup brine reserved
¼	teaspoon freshly ground pepper

Sandwiches

6	individual French bread rolls, sliced in half lengthwise
¾	pound prosciutto, sliced
¾	pound provolone cheese, sliced
½	pound Genoa salami, sliced
	Olive oil for brushing grill rack

For salad, mix together oil and garlic in a large bowl. Toss with cauliflower, broccoli, green pepper, onion, and olives. Mix in olive brine and pepper. Toss vegetables again and cover lightly. Refrigerate overnight.

Prepare the grill, and while the coals are heating, prepare the sandwiches. Chop marinated vegetables in food processor fitted with steel blade. After three or four pulses, they will be finely chopped. Spoon salad over rolls. Layer meats and cheese over vegetables. Wrap each sandwich in a double thickness of aluminum foil.

When coals are hot, place sandwiches on grill and cook for about 3 minutes, turning sandwiches after 1½ minutes. Cheese will have melted, and sandwich will be hot.

Serve sandwiches hot, allowing guests to unwrap the sandwiches themselves.

Open-Face Grilled
Pepper Sandwiches

8 servings

8   slices Italian bread
    Olive oil or canola oil for brushing grill rack
1   large Vidalia onion, sliced
1   medium-sized red bell pepper, seeded and sliced
1   medium-sized yellow pepper, seeded and sliced
¼   cup capers, including liquid
2   tablespoons olive oil or canola oil
1   2-ounce can flat anchovy fillets, drained

Prepare the grill, and when the coals are hot, toast bread on a grill rack, brushed with oil, about 4 to 6 inches from heat source, for 2 minutes on each side or until lightly browned. Transfer to a serving plate.

Brush rack with oil again. Grill onions and peppers for about 5 minutes, turning once or twice and brushing with oil as necessary. Vegetables will begin to char and be tender. Spoon vegetables into a bowl and toss with capers and 2 tablespoons oil. Mound vegetable mixture on warm toast. Lay an anchovy on top of each sandwich and serve hot.

GRAZING PARTY

A grazing party is perfect for the Fourth of July, dinner on the patio, a Labor Day celebration, or any other occasion when you are entertaining. This menu can be adapted for any number of guests.

Menu

Roasted Chestnuts
Smoked Shrimp Dip
Smoked Brats with Caramelized Red Onions
Chicken Kabobs on Italian Bread
Dessert Pizza or Fresh Fruit

Roasted Chestnuts

6 servings

36   chestnuts

Prepare the grill.

Using a small, sharp knife, cut an X, about ½ inch long, into each chestnut. Wrap chestnuts, in groups of 6, in aluminum foil and, when coals are hot, place packages on grill. Cook about 45 minutes, turning aluminum packages every 15 minutes. Chestnuts will be tender when done. Open the packages, and when the chestnuts are cool enough, your guests can peel and eat them.

Smoked Shrimp Dip

Use crudités such as carrots, scallions, celery sticks, and broccoli florets and crackers for dipping.

8 servings

⅓	cup chili sauce
1	teaspoon chili powder
¼	teaspoon ground cumin
¾	pound large shrimp, peeled and deveined
3	cups mesquite chips, soaked in cold water for 1 hour and drained
¾	pound part-skim ricotta cheese
½	pound cream cheese at room temperature
3	scallions, minced
3	ribs celery, minced
¼	teaspoon garlic powder

Prepare smoker according to manufacturer's directions.

While the coals are heating, mix together chili sauce, chili powder, and cumin. Add shrimp to sauce and make sure they are well coated. Let shrimp marinate until coals are hot.

When coals are hot, sprinkle with drained wood. Using pot holders, set water pan, about two-thirds full of hot water, in place. Set shrimp on grill and cover. Smoke shrimp for about 30 minutes. When cooked, shrimp will become opaque.

Transfer shrimp to a bowl. In a blender or processor puree ricotta cheese, cream cheese, scallions, celery, and garlic powder. Chop shrimp and add them, including the chili sauce. Mix well. Spoon into a serving bowl. Cover and refrigerate until serving time. Stir before serving.

Smoked Brats with Caramelized Red Onions

8 servings

2	tablespoons canola oil
3	tablespoons margarine or butter
3	cloves garlic, minced
3	large red onions, sliced thin
¼	cup firmly packed light brown sugar
½	teaspoon salt
¼	teaspoon freshly ground black pepper
½	teaspoon dried rosemary
3	cups mesquite chips, soaked in cold water for 1 hour and drained
8	bratwurst
	Stone-ground mustard
	Pickles

Heat oil and margarine in a large frying pan over medium heat. Add garlic and onions and sauté, stirring occasionally, until onions are soft, about 4 to 5 minutes. Stir in brown sugar, salt, pepper, and rosemary. Continue cooking 4 to 5 minutes. Do not let onions turn brown. Remove onions from heat and set aside.

Prepare a smoker according to manufacturer's directions. When coals are hot, add drained wood. Using pot holders, set the water pan, about two-thirds full of hot water, in place.

Prick the bratwurst with a fork about three times and set on grill. Cover and smoke for about 45 minutes. They will be a golden color and cooked through. Remove brats and cut into 1-inch pieces. Arrange pieces of brats with toothpicks on a serving dish. Serve with a dish of mustard, a bowl of pickles, and the caramelized onions, reheated if necessary.

Chicken Kabobs on Italian Bread

Herb stems are used as skewers in this recipe.

6 servings

Italian Marinade

1¼	cups olive oil
1¼	cups red wine vinegar
2	tablespoons freshly squeezed lemon juice
1	tablespoon grated lemon zest
3	cloves garlic, minced
2	tablespoons chopped fresh mint
¾	teaspoon dried oregano

1½	pounds boneless, skinless chicken breast, cut into 1-inch pieces
	Enough Italian bread for 6 sandwiches
	Lettuce leaves
	Sliced tomatoes

Soak six bamboo skewers in cold water for 15 minutes; drain. Or use six oregano or mint stems, all leaves removed and one end shaped into a point.

Combine marinade ingredients in a bowl. Pour marinade evenly into two large self-sealing plastic bags. Divide chicken pieces and place in bags. Seal bags securely. Turn bags several times so that all chicken pieces are touched by marinade. Place bags in a shallow glass dish and marinate in refrigerator for 3 to 4 hours, turning occasionally.

Prepare the grill, and when the coals are hot, drain chicken and reserve marinade as a brushing sauce. Thread chicken pieces onto skewers. Wrap aluminum foil around tips of herb skewers to prevent scorching. Set kabobs on grill rack about 4 to 6 inches from heat source. Grill kabobs for about 9 minutes, turning and brushing with reserved marinade every 3 minutes. Chicken is done when juices run clear when meat is pierced with a fork. Do not overcook; chicken will become tough. Warm bread on the grill, cut side down, for 1 to 2 minutes, until lightly toasted and warm.

Remove the chicken from the grill and set on a tray. Bring chicken to the table hot. Have guests make their own sandwiches by removing chicken from skewers and placing it on the bread. Serve with lettuce and sliced tomatoes.

Dessert Pizza

For best results, make sure the pizza tiles are hot before adding the dessert pizza.

12 to 16 servings

1	recipe pizza dough (see Index)
4	(enough to cover crust, leaving ½-inch border) cooking apples such as Granny Smith, peeled and sliced thin
3	tablespoons freshly squeezed lemon juice
¼	cup sugar
½	teaspoon ground cinnamon

With floured hands, push dough evenly into two round circles about 9 to 10 inches in diameter or roll out dough on a lightly floured pastry cloth with a rolling pin.

Place apples in a deep bowl. Toss with lemon juice, sugar, and cinnamon.

Prepare the grill, and when the coals are hot, arrange fruit on pizza crust. Place barbecue pizza tray, set with tiles, on the grill. When tiles are hot, shift pizza onto a pizza paddle and then onto the heated tiles, cooking one pizza at a time. Cover grill and cook. When cooked, pizza crust will be firm and topping will be hot. It should take 5 to 10 minutes.

APPENDIX

For the British Cook

In the United States, cooks use standard measuring cups and spoons, but in Great Britain the measuring devices vary from one kitchen to the next, and there is no such thing as a standard "cup." The U.S. and Britain have the same solid measurements, but liquids can be confusing. Below is a chart that should help British cooks use my recipes. Please keep in mind that the equivalents are approximate. As always, let your tastebuds be your guide.

BRITISH	AMERICAN
1 quart	2½ pints
1 pint	1¼ pints
½ pint (1 gill)	10 fluid ounces (1¼ cups)
¼ pint	5 fluid ounces (⅝ cup)
1 tablespoon	1⅛ tablespoons
1 dessertspoon	1 tablespoon
1 teaspoon	⅓ fluid ounces

AMERICAN	BRITISH
1 quart	1½ pints + 3 tbs. (32 fluid ounces)
1 pint	¾ pint + 2 tbs. (16 fluid ounces)
1 cup	½ pint − 2 tbs. (8 fluid ounces)

INDEX